The New Americans
Recent Immigration and American Society

Edited by
Steven J. Gold and Rubén G. Rumbaut

A Series from LFB Scholarly

Asian Indian Professionals
The Culture of Success

Sabeen Sandhu

LFB Scholarly Publishing LLC
El Paso 2012

Library of Congress Cataloging-in-Publication Data

Sandhu, Sabeen, 1977-
   Asian Indian professionals : the culture of success / Sabeen Sandhu.
      p. cm. -- (The new Americans)
   Includes bibliographical references and index.
   ISBN 978-1-59332-522-0 (hardcover : alk. paper)
   1. East Indians--United States. 2. Professional employees--United
States. 3. Success in business--United States. I. Title.
   E184.E2S26 2012
   973.0491'4--dc23
                                        2012021388

ISBN 978-1-59332-522-0

Table of Contents

Acknowledgements

From start to finish, this book involves so many people. It began with an idea back in the winter of 2003 in Calvin Morrill and David Snow's Field Methods seminar at the University of California, Irvine. Nearly ten years later, the idea evolved into this book – *Asian Indian Professionals: The Culture of Success*.

I am incredibly grateful to the following people for their sociological insights and suggestions during various stages of writing this book: Calvin Morrill, Jennifer Lee, Frank Bean, Susan Brown, Leo Chavez, Sandra Chiaramonte, Dan Dexheimer, Anke Schulz, David Snow, Joy Pixley, Cynthia Feliciano, Rubén G. Rumbaut, Alma Garcia, Matt Huffman, Adrian Favell, Wang Feng, Marilyn Fernandez, Sarah Thompson, Chunyan Song, Mike Ballen, Gloria Hofer, Monica Trieu, Laura Nichols, Christine Oh, and Charles Morgan. Many of their comments and suggestions are included in this book and have made it a better publication.

I also appreciate the opportunity to publish this book in The New Americans series through LFB Scholarly Press. I thank Leo Balk, Steven J. Gold, and Rubén G. Rumbaut for their review of my manuscript and inclusion in a series committed to understanding how immigration is changing the United States.

Part of the research that this book is based on is funded by the School of Social Sciences Regents Dissertation and Writing Fellowship and the Frank Lynch Endowment. I thank the University of California at Irvine's Graduate Committee, Dean Barbara Dosher, and Mr. Frank Lynch for their generous contribution and insightful comments regarding this research.

I also thank the participants of this study for their incredible generosity. Despite their very busy lives, they saw the importance of a study on the culture of success among Asian Indian elites. I thank them for letting me into their lives and allowing me to share them in this book.

My deepest thanks to my family: Sukhdev, Lovleen, Suneet, Jodi, Chloe, and Manny. Your immigration experiences fuel my interest in the subject. I dedicate this book to you.

CHAPTER ONE

Introduction: Asian Indian Professionals in the Silicon Valley and Southern California

"We need a language that would encompass several categories of Indians who have been overlooked, even in recent histories of the Indian diasporas, and whose experiences reasonably stretch the perhaps already overextended reach of the word 'diaspora'."

-- Vinay Lal (2008: 127)

"I don't think that you're going to find poverty here. Oh, that's your point...."

-- Sid, 42 year old, Venture Capitalist

Although international migrants account for barely three percent of the world's population, they have an incredible impact on the world.[1] For example, take labor migrants from the Third World; they have historically contributed to the development of first world nations. Despite this pivotal role in development, international migrants are often marginalized in their receiving countries and oscillate between being a social problem and social solution (Mills 1994). Much of this has to do with misconceptions about international migrants. Rumbaut

---

[1] Rubén G. Rumbaut (2008) explains that ninety-seven percent of the world's population continues to live in their country of birth. It is only 191 million, or a little under three percent, that engage in international migration (72).

1

(2008: 72) correctly notes that popular myths about immigrants often trounce empirical realities:

Contemporary nativism, in the current political climate, rails against immigration without caring to understand the history and complexity of the flows, the forces that propel it, the networks that sustain it, or the demographic dynamics that will the American and global futures. In doing so it exemplifies the definition of a delusion.
At a basic level, for example, the general public is likely to be surprised that international migrants account for such a small percent of the world's population. They often estimate the population to be significantly larger because the United States is the primary destination of international migrants who tend to settle in particular regions of the nation.

This is true of high-skilled Asian Indian migrants in the United States. Scholars often let the statistics of this group speak for themselves. Based on current data from the U.S. Census and the Department of Homeland Security's Office of Immigration Statistics (OIS), the U.S. is home to approximately 2.3 million residents of Indian ancestry. Of this figure, 1.6 million are foreign-born or immigrants, while about half a million are U.S. born.[2] While their history of migration dates back to 1790, the population remained relatively small until the 1990s.[3] In fact, slightly over forty percent Asian Indian immigrants arrived in the U.S. over the last decade largely due to family reunification provisions in immigration law as well as the demand for high skilled laborers. Today, the majority of the Asian Indian population resides in four states: California, New Jersey, New York, and Texas. Data from the 2010 U.S. Census reveals that Asian Indians have high rates of educational attainment, labor market performance, and average earnings. Moreover, the fact that Asian

---

[2] In this book I define the foreign born as the U.S. Census does – individuals who did not have U.S. citizenship at birth (naturalized citizens, permanent residents, refugees/asylees, visa holders, and unauthorized migrants). I use the term foreign born and immigrant interchangeably.

[3] Historical documents reveal that the first Asian Indian to visit the United States was a South Indian who visited Massachusetts in 1790. The purpose of his visit was for commerce between India and the United States. However, more sizable streams of migration occurred later, around 1895, when Punjabis who were in Canada migrated south to the work in California's agricultural industry (Sahoo et al 2010).

Indians statistically outperform other migrants, racial and ethnic groups, and even U.S. citizens makes their study seem unwarranted and unnecessary.

This is because the scholarship on international migration is dominated by studies on low-skilled migrants, immigrant entrepreneurs, and their impact on the black urban underclass. Because most scholars treat migration as a social problem, they have long examined the paradoxes of ethnic poverty and immigrant mobility. As a result theoretical developments are often made within the paradigm of migration as a social problem. Scholars continue to extend classical theories on assimilation (Warner and Srole 1945; Park 1950; Gordon 1964), human capital acquisition (Mincer 1974; Piore 1979; Chiswick 1977; Borjas 1985), and industrial restructuring (Wilson 1987; Waldinger 1996; 1997) to contemporary quandaries of migration. But what about the other end—migration as a social solution? In the sense that many institutions of higher learning, corporations, and nations rely on high skilled migrants for economic growth and an edge in global competitiveness, migration is a social solution (Swift 2010; Pepitone 2011). However, even nascent scholarship on the migration of the highly skilled continues to focus on it as a social problem. The question of whether Asian Indian immigrant professionals compete with their native-born American counterparts for jobs dominates research (Alarcon 1999; Cornelius, Espenshade, and Salehyan 2001; Loftstrom 2001; Lowell 2001; Usdansky and Espenshade 2001; Batalova 2006; Sahoo et al 2010).

Beyond these issues of statistical "success" and labor market competition, little else is known about these high skilled migrants themselves. Low skilled first generation migrants quickly accommodate to their new situation in the United States for survival. High skilled migrants, on the other hand, have educational, employment, and income parity to the native majority and engage in the more subtle and gradual process assimilation.[4] In addition, most

---

[4] Theories of cultural assimilation (Park and Burgess 1924; Warner and Srole 1945; Gordon 1964; Portes and Zhou 1993; Zhou 1999) forward that accommodation is the modal adaptation of first generation adult immigrants, while assimilation is the modal outcome for only young, malleable, second generation migrants. While first generation adult migrants economically,

high skilled migrants are employed in corporations, know for their racial, social, and gender homogeneity that compel social conformity (Moore 1962; Kanter 1977; Cabezas et al. 1986; Morrill 1995; Woo 2000; Saxenian 2001).[5] In the corporate world, human capital differences between high skilled migrants and native-born professionals are negligible. With this skill homogeneity, subtle differences in their culture become more meaningful and are the basis of exclusion (Veblen 1899; Collins 1979; Lamont 1992). Collins (1979) appropriately notes that education does not train people for occupation success, so it is an invalid predictor of occupational mobility. Accordingly, the roles of social and cultural capital are more salient than socioeconomic factors in the adaptation and assimilation of high skilled migrants.[6] And the understanding of how so was the original motivation for this research.

INITIAL RESEARCH FOCUS

Despite being a socioeconomic success story, many Asian Indian high skilled migrants perceive exclusion in the corporate workplace and believe that this constrains their occupational mobility (Cabezas et al. 1986; AACI 1993; Tang 1993; Chang and Yang 1996; Fernandez 1998; Prashad 2000; Woo 2000; Saxenian 2001; Sandhu 2002; 2003). Scholars (Tang 1996; Fernandez 1998; Saxenian 1999) who pursue

---

politically, socially, and culturally accommodate to life in the United States, only the second generation are able to assimilate at the primary group level.

[5] Moore (1962), Kanter (1977), and Morrill (1995) find that corporations engage in the monoethnic reproduction of executives when hiring: in this largely male and white world, minorities must "fit in" with the behavior and speech styles of European-American male executives.

[6] Social capital is the capacity to command concrete or intangible resources on an individual and group level by virtue of membership in social networks or social institutions (Loury 1977; Bourdieu 1986; Portes and Zhou 1992; Portes 1995; 1998). Social capital is manifest through sets of obligations, shared norms, and mutual trust necessary to accomplish actions. Cultural capital is more symbolic and refers to the distinctive tastes and lifestyles that serve as status markers which simultaneously structure inclusion and exclusion (Passeron and Bourdieu 1977; Lamont 1992). Cultural capital includes linguistic competence, command of high culture, displays of cultivated dispositions, level of education, intelligence, and self-actualization. Cultural capital is a major basis for exclusion in the United States; those who are not socialized into these aesthetics are often excluded from high status groups.

studies on glass ceilings—subtle forms of discrimination or institutional barriers to mobility based on race—rely on income data and find little evidence in support of this hypothesis. If this perception of exclusion is not evident in income data, then a qualitative examination of culture is warranted. How is it that cultural differences are transformed into inequality? And conversely, how can culture be used as an adaptive strategy to perceived inequality?

The best mode to systematically examine culture is ethnography. Ethnography, as defined by Weich (1985: 368), is the "sustained, explicit, methodical observation and paraphrasing of social situations in relation to their natural occurring contexts (Morrill and Fine 1997). This method allows ethnographers to engage in systematic observation and capture the meaning of subjects' actions as understood by subjects themselves (Blumer 1969; Katz 1997). Beginning with these wide research questions and the ethnographic method, I found a suitable research site to observe Asian Indian high skilled migrants in their natural setting—a professional organization that I refer to as *Skilled Speakers International.* This research focuses on two research sites within this international professional organization: (1) The *Indian Professional Skilled Speakers* club in Southern California; and (2) The *Indian Communicators* club in California's Silicon Valley. Both of these specialized clubs were founded by and cater to Asian Indian professionals.

Most social science research is conducted deductively. Scholars begin with a research question and construct a fitting research design. Ethnography is the opposite; ethnographers work inductively and forgo research questions. They let data drive all aspects of a study. I detailed my original motives for this research above. Again, I entered the field with a research proposal intent on answering three questions: (1) how do Asian Indians adapt to economic and social life in the United States; (2) what barriers, if any, do they face in the United States labor market; and (3) what role do mediating organizations and social and cultural capital play in their adaptation and assimilation?

Despite articulating these research questions, several weeks of complete participant observation issues yielded few answers. In fact, even when interviewing by comment, the majority of Asian Indian club members reported that they had not experienced discrimination in the labor market or even perceived a sense of exclusion. The closest experience that they came to experiencing discrimination were ignorant comments made by American colleagues about the lack of development in India or stories from their Asian Indian friends and acquaintances about their own experiences with discrimination. For example, *Gary,* a successful engineer turned executive, recalled an American colleague asking him whether there were automobiles in India. He had assumed that India was as developed as the Disney cartoon, *Jungle Book,* depicted. He was under the assumption that *Gary* rode a camel or elephant to work.

Irman, a retired chief executive officer of a global information technology company turned angel investor, argued that those who feel discriminated against or perceive exclusion are actually frustrated with the mobility prospects of technical careers. He experienced this in his own professional development, but asserted that reaching a plateau in his career was the natural progression in a technology career and not due to discrimination. *Irman* elaborates, "I was only thirty-five and I had become the most senior technology person. I had reached the limit of what is possible. It bothered me that there was no other place for me and this was where I'd be for the rest of my life."

Shalin, the chief technology office of a prominent accounting and tax firm, agrees with *Irman,* but notes that the U.S. labor market is far more meritocratic than India's. He also notes that American employees have greater resources at their disposal to complete their job tasks and deliverables. *Shalin* suggests that because of this, even if highly skilled Asian Indian migrants encounter discrimination in the United States, they would disregard it or not even notice because they are treated far worse in India. He explains,

> You have to understand something—there is a very big difference in the way that employees are treated as far as— well, I mean I think there's just more effort put in. It is tremendous because Indian employees usually don't have enough resources in respect to fixing problems. Employees usually spend twenty-four hours just fixing something and there's no overtime. Plus you are still expected to come into work the next day bright and early.

Beyond working with limited resources, *Shalin* argues that the labor market in India is far more competitive than in the United States. He continues, "Competition is generally prevalent in Indian society at large. I don't think that it is intentional, but because of the situation where you have to be at the top to make it in school in India. There are just too many people competing for too few college positions or even too few jobs." This is ironic, since a key concern over the migration of the highly skilled concerns whether they compete with or displace native-born American workers.

Suresh also stresses the meritocratic nature of the U.S. labor market. Even in highly competitive entrepreneurial ventures, skills speak for themselves. He elaborates, "Zero. Zero discrimination. I have not felt it. Not even in my business deals. If anything it is about your competency, how good you are, what you have to provide, your service that you can provide. Nothing based on my race that I have been left behind or I can complain and say because I am Indian I can't make progress. It would be my lack of ability, nothing else."

SHIFTING APPROACH AND FOCUS

After noting these observational insights, I decided to stop thinking deductively and allow induction to take over. Instead of forcing the data to fit my hypothesis, I focused on the fundamental question that ethnographies uncover: what is really going on in the research situation (Glaser and Strauss 1967; Malinowski 1967; Blumer 1969; Glaser 1992; Snow and Anderson 1993; Morrill 1995; Katz 1997; Morrill and Fine 1997; Goodwin 2002; Snow, Morrill, and Anderson 2003; Loftland et al 2006)?

What the research situation objectively presented was a window into the day-to-day activities of highly skilled and extremely successful Asian Indians migrants. Because the majority of the members of *Skilled Speakers International* are pioneers in the medical, entertainment, information technology, and defense industries, they constitute elites. Beyond their phenomenal occupational feats, many have developed technologies, pharmaceuticals, and made other contributions that revolutionized the world. Observing and also experiencing various aspects of their professional, public, and private lives revealed volumes about the real habits highly successful Asian Indian immigrants and the meaning of their culture of success. Therefore, the data presented two, more appropriate, lines of inquiry for this book: (1) how do highly successful Asian Indian elites understand their own success; and (2) how does culture benefit and constrain their everyday lives? Instead of focusing on the barriers that Asian Indian elites encounter and their resulting adaptive strategies, the data presented the opposite—how do Asian Indian elites understand and cope with their success? The next five chapters of this book provide answers to these questions based on three years of complete participant observation in both research sites, forty-four in-depth interviews with club members and a comparison group of non-members, and an analysis of data from the 2000 Integrated Public Use Microdata Series (IPUMS).

WHY STUDY ASIAN INDIAN ELITES?

In spite of understanding that one of the fundamental tasks of sociology is to examine empirically assess implicit assumptions (Durkheim 1893), many express great skepticism over the analytical payoff of studying outliers. As prior mentioned, data from both the 2000 and 2010 U.S. Censuses capture the remarkable success of Asian Indian migrants. They have high rates of educational attainment, labor market performance, average earnings over sixty thousand dollars per year, and high rates of marriage that exceed other migrants, racial and ethnic groups, and their native born counterparts. Although Asian Indians are an overall success, this book focuses on an even smaller subset of this population—elites. There are approximately two hundred thousand Asian Indian millionaires in the United States. They comprise ten percent of U.S. millionaires and are the focus of this research.

As I later elaborate in chapter two, the study of these "outliers" is a methodological strategy. They constitute a critical case study, in the sense that they are a strategic research sample (Merton 1987; Becker 1992; Ragin and Becker 1992; Portes 1995; Morrill and Fine 1997; Foner, Rumbaut, and Gold 2000; Goodwin and Horowitz 2002; Lieberson 2002). As the chapters of this book nicely reveal, the study of Asian Indian elites extends sociological theory beyond immigration. The study of this atypical group clearly illuminates how the labor market functions, how the processes of assimilation take place, and how identity is constructed.

At a more basic level, however, there are numerous misconceptions about this group of international migrants. Just as Morrill (1995: 9) gets behind the folk-hero status of executives through his ethnography on conflict management in corporations, this research gets behind the model minority myth as it applies to Asian Indian elites. For example, their success is often curiously attributed to biology, luck, or other external factors. Curiously, as I point out in chapter three, Asian Indian elites often buy into such misconceptions. Ultimately, this critical case study is as a useful exercise in sociology as it documents the empirical reality of their success, challenges *a priori* ideas, and extends assimilation, social and cultural capital, symbolic interactionism, and immigration concepts and theories.

THE STRUCTURE OF THIS BOOK

This introduction briefly touches on theoretical and methodological motivations of my research, including relevant literature on economic incorporation and immigration, symbolic capital, and the particular cultural, economic, and demographic contexts of Asian Indian immigrants. The next chapter, on research methods, elaborates on many of issues raised in this introduction. It details the making of an analytic ethnography (including my access sampling, and analysis strategies) and addresses the management of gender relations in the field, particularly the gender stereotypes I had to negotiate vis-à-vis my informants.

Chapter three examines the scripts of success Asian Indian elites use in their everyday lives. How they come to define and understand their own success speaks volumes about their adaptive strategies and the construction of a culture of success. Chapter four uncovers the role of spouses in elite success. This chapter also addresses how gender relations vary between Los Angeles and the Silicon Valley. The final empirical chapter, chapter five, examines the role of the new second generation in the culture of success. Just as with their spouses, the meaning of success for Asian Indian elites is negotiated through the mobility of their children. Chapter six, the conclusion, addresses the immigration and workplace policy implications that this book raises. It also addresses directions for future research.

CHAPTER TWO

Ethnographic Research Methods: Negotiating Race, Class, and Gender in the Field

"The student is thrown into the ethnographic ocean, and nature takes its course. If he is worth his salt, he will return from the field [a sociologist]. "
--Nader (1970: 114)

"In fact, the richness of the data in qualitative studies often permits a variety of analyses and interpretations—something that can be quite frustrating to researchers. "
--Goodwin and Horowitz (1992: 43)

These ethnographers (Nader 1970; Goodwin and Horowitz 1970) make apt remarks about ethnographic research: allowing data to drive all aspects of a study, from the research questions, methods, to theory extension, can be a daunting proposition. While the sciences have a deductive bent, ethnographers forgo such hypothesis testing and let induction guide their research (Glaser and Strauss 1967; Glaser 1992; Snow, Morrill, and Anderson 2003; Loftland et al 2006). This is why ethnographic research is often full of surprises, profound, and a testament to empiricism (Durkheim 1895, 1912; Morrill and Fine 1997; Goodwin and Horowitz 2002). However, letting nature, or in this case data, take its course is often easier said than done.

Although poised to let data drive all aspects of my analytic ethnography, I still entered the research situation thinking deductively and had a theoretically informed hypothesis in mind. As elaborated in the introduction, I hoped to address how professional organizations are an adaptive strategy for Asian Indian professionals who encounter barriers in the labor market. Yet my initial observations yielded minimal data on labor market barriers, exclusion, and resulting adaptive strategies. Instead of forcing the data to fit my hypothesis, I focused on the fundamental question that ethnographies uncover: what is really going on in the research situation (Glaser and Strauss 1967; Malinowski 1967; Blumer 1969; Glaser 1992; Snow and Anderson 1993; Morrill 1995; Katz 1997; Morrill and Fine 1997; Goodwin 2002; Snow, Morrill, and Anderson 2003; Loftland et al 2006)?

After several weeks of note taking, interviewing by comment, coding, and drafting preliminary memos, my drive to deduce finally relented. What the research situation objectively presented was a window into the day-to-day activities of highly successful Asian Indian elites. Observing and also experiencing various aspects of their professional, public, and private lives revealed volumes about the real habits highly successful Asian Indian immigrants and the meaning of their culture of success. Therefore, the data presented two, more appropriate, lines of inquiry for this book: (1) how do highly successful Asian Indian elites understand their own success; and (2) how does culture benefit and constrain their everyday lives?

This chapter documents how I arrive at answers to these specific research questions. In line with the principles of grounded theory, this emergent research agenda required an emergent multi-method research design. Part one of this chapter details the objective aspects of my research methods, while part two concerns the more subjective aspects of managing my role as a researcher.

RESEARCH METHODS

An Emergent Research Design

As addressed above, this book originated from research methods—ethnography. Ethnography, as defined by Weick (1985: 368), is the "sustained, explicit, methodical observation and paraphrasing of social situations in relation to their natural occurring contexts (Morrill and Fine 1997). Put otherwise, through systematic observation ethnographers capture the meaning of subjects' actions to subjects (Blumer 1969; Katz 1997). This is why this is an appropriate method to study culture, as there are tangible and tacit aspects to it.

I began with a method, found a research site, and let data drive all subsequent aspects of this study.[7] Scholars suggest that emergent phenomena are best studied ethnographically (Glaser and Straus 1967; Glaser 1992; Loftland et al 2006). This being the case, ethnographers employ flexible research methods because they encounter methodological issues and choices at every stage of the emergent research process (Morrill and Fine 1997; Goodwin and Horowtiz 2002).

While ethnography is the primary research method of this study, at specific stages of the research process additional methods are employed as well. Denzin (1989) argues that social reality is far too complex and multifaceted to be adequately grasped by and single method. He recommends that researchers combine, complement, and supplement their strategies to methodologically triangulate to the truth. Heeding Denzin's advice, and because the research questions at the heart of this book emerged from the field, this study logically draws on multiple methodologies and data sources. For example, of all the empirical chapters of this book are primarily based on participant observation, but are also supplemented with a significant amount of interview data. In addition to these qualitative methods, chapter four includes quantitative data from the 2000 Integrated Public Use Microdata Series (IPUMS).

Sample Selection—A Critical Case Study

A critical case study is an in-depth, multifaceted investigation or a single social phenomenon that is an instance of a broader happening (Feagin, Sjoberg, and Orum 1991; Snow and Anderson 1991; Ragin and Becker 1992; Goodwin and Horowitz 2002). This ethnography is a critical case study of Asian Indian elites in a professional organization. This case study is critical in the sense that it is a strategic research site (Merton 1987; 1995). This single case is illustrative of the construction of a culture of success among Asian Indian elites and its wider consequences. Studying Asian Indian elites at the level of a professional organization that allows entrée into their often hard to access profession, public, and private worlds, grounds the observation

---

[7] This book originated in Professors Calvin Morrill and David A. Snow's 2003-2004 Field Methods seminar at the University of California, Irvine. The seminar was fruitful as I developed my ideas for this now published book.

of them in their natural surroundings, and ultimately allows researchers to understand them holistically (Feagin, Orum, and Sjoberg 1991; Ragin and Becker 1992; Goodwin and Horowitz 2002; Lieberson 2002).

Critics of the case study method charge that it is unreliable, unrepresentative, reactive, and not replicable (Katz 1997). However, the goal of social science research—to present the empirical reality of social life—is unachievable without it. Other scholars (Snow and Anderson 1991; Ragin and Becker 1992; Katz 1997; Morrill and Fine 1997; Goodwin and Horowitz 2002) extol the virtues of the case study method. For example, case studies provide proof of the lived experiences of people. This methodological strategy allows social scientists the opportunity to study socially curious phenomena at a relatively small price; usually, one researcher can perform systematic observations with great richness and depth (Feagin, Sjoberg, and Orum 1991).

While critics also argue that the small number of cases in the case study approach impedes theory extension and generalization, this is not the case. Sometimes few instances of a social phenomenon exist and the only way to study them is the case study approach. This is the case with Asian Indian elites; how else can they be systematically observed in their natural surroundings over time? As mentioned in the introduction, there are few studies on Asian Indian elites. Also, the majority of these studies are quantitative. While, these studies provide gross overviews of the incorporation of Asian Indians in the United States, they reveal little about their actual lives. Rather than providing statistical data on a cross-section of individuals, a critical case study allows researchers to get at the nuances of this group and understand the processes fundamental to their lives (Snow and Anderson 1991). [8] Again, a case study is a good methodological strategy.

Even with small numbers, case studies lend themselves to theory extension and generation because they provide more complex and nuanced understandings of social life (Feagin, Sjoberg, and Orum

---

[8] Manalansan (2000: 2) explains that the potential of ethnography has been overlooked in Asian American Studies: "While literary, quantitative, and historical analyses enable sweeping views of social life, they are unable to go beyond an abstract and distant vantage point." This critical case study and multi-sited ethnography is a closer inspection of the real life activities of Asian Indian elites.

1991; Ragin and Becker 1992).[9] In agreement, Morrill and Fine (1997) argue that we must expand our understanding generalizability to include providing additive depth, theoretical generalizability; and the naturalistic generalizability of findings, or whether they resonate with readers (Morrill and Fine 1997: 440-441). Hence, studying Asian Indian elites with the case study approach yields empirical, theoretical, and experiential fruits.

Data Collection: Complete Participant Observation, Ethnographic Interviews, and Descriptive Statistics

As addressed in the introduction, the population of Asian Indians is concentrated in two regions of California: (1) the Los Angeles/Orange County area; and (2) Santa Clara County. While I could have snowball sampled Asian Indian elites from both of these regions and conducted in-depth interviews with them, my findings would capture their experiences at one particular moment in time and overlook the everyday contexts that Asian Indian elites encounter. My study would be just another gross overview of Asian Indian elites in the United States. Working ethnographically, however, allows for a deeper understanding of Asian Indian elites as they can be observed over time and within the contexts that they encounter on a daily basis. Beyond the workplace, it is difficult to pinpoint the actually contexts that this elusive population encounters. Unlike low-skilled migrant groups that cluster in ethnic enclaves, Asian Indian elites do not. They are economically mobile, more likely to live in integrated neighborhoods, and intermarry at higher rates (Massey and Denton 1992; Farley 1996; Hirschman et al 1999).

After quickly perusing the business pages of the *Los Angeles Times, San Jose Mercury News,* and *India West,* Asian Indian elites seemed to frequent professional organizations as keynote speakers, invited guests, or members. Because these activities often occur after work hours, they reveal the intersection of the professional, public, and personal lives of Asian Indian elites. Therefore, discovering a

---

[9] Feagin, Sjoberg, and Odum (1991) explain that the case study approach is a downplayed and neglected research method. While scholars favor large samples for reliability, validity, and theory extension, case studies offer reliability, validity, and theoretical generalizability on a deeper level.

mainstream professional organization that caters to Asian Indian elites in Southern California and the Silicon Valley was a research goldmine. And, as I began my research with a method—ethnography—I required such a research site.

Therein lies the methodological warrant for conducting a multi-sited ethnography on *Skilled Speakers International*. *Skilled Speakers International* was founded in 1924 in Southern California to provide training in communication and leadership to the community. The organization made its community mission global and now boasts over 9,300 clubs in over eighty countries with over 200,000 members. The most significant growth in the organization of *Skilled Speakers International* is in corporate sponsored clubs that exist on company sites. More than one thousand major organizations sponsor "in house" clubs that offer training and workshops to their employees. These companies range from information technology companies like the Intel Corporation and Microsoft, to agencies within the U.S. government like the Department of Justice and the Food and Drug Administration, and even the University of California, an educational institution. This growth suggests that *Skilled Speakers International*, a non-profit, voluntary professional organization, is becoming institutionalized within corporate America. Moreover, many companies require that their sales and public relations staff become members of on-site or off-site *Skilled Speakers International clubs.*

Skilled Speakers International is becoming popular among immigrants too. Two Asian Indian elites founded specialized clubs that cater to the population of Asian Indian professionals. These clubs are curiously located where Asian Indians are geographically concentrated—Southern California and the Silicon Valley.[10] While their stated goal is no different than *Skilled Speakers International*, to

---

[10] As documented in the introduction, data from the both the 2000 and 2010 US Censuses reveal that Asian Indians are the fastest growing ethnic group in the United States. Over the past decade, they Indian immigrant population doubled in ten states. Most Indians concentrate in two of California's metropolitan areas: (1) the San Jose-Sunnyvale-Santa Clara; and (2) Los Angeles-Long Beach-Santa Ana. These residential concentrations coincide with three industries that many Asian Indians have developed and are employed in: (1) Los Angeles' entertainment technology industry; (2) Silicon Valley's Information technology industry; and (3) Orange County's defense and information technology industry (Milken Institute 2003; Terrazas et al 2010; U.S. Census 2000; 2010).

foster communication and leadership skills, my task as a ethnographer was to assess what is really going on there.

This organization provides convenient access to Asian Indian elites in Southern California and the Silicon Valley. As Katz (1997) and Morrill (1995) note, getting behind the scenes of the social worlds of the elite and the admired, is a compelling reason to conduct an ethnography. Just as Morrill (1995) gets behind the folk hero status of executives in American society and explains how conflict is managed in corporation, this study gets behind elite status and uncovers how a culture of success is constructed and becomes consequential for Asian Indian elites.

While Katz (1997: 402) disagrees, I argue that are legitimate obstacles to studying elites. While their achievements are well known, the organizations that elites work for guard them with tenacity and often deter outsiders from contacting them. Beyond this status issue, elites often have rigorous time schedules that hinder studies on them. And even when interviews are granted, researchers face the challenging task of disentangling the elite from the formal corporate scripts and prepared public relations responses that the often recount (Thomas 1995).[11] This ethnography is a means around this; Asian Indian elites are observable for an extended period of time in their natural setting.

Between 2003 and 2006, I did just this and conducted participant observation in two research sites: (1) the *Indian Professional Skilled Speakers Club* in Southern California; and (2) the *Indian Communicators Skilled Speakers Club* in California's Silicon Valley. In the *Indian Professional Skilled Speakers Club* in Southern California, an average of thirty members and guests, most of whom were men, spent every Tuesday evening toasting to life, commenting on current events, and speaking about their professional, public, and private lives in accordance to the guidelines of *Skilled Speakers International.* Paid members followed the *Skilled Speakers International Education Program* where they complete a series of manuals that cultivate communication and leadership skills. Members also attended competitions, training programs, and events hosted by

---

[11] Thomas (1995) explains that elites have a three-fold persona: (1) individual; (2) position; and (3) organizational. If solely relying on an interview, the researcher must separate each persona. Through participant observation and interviews, the elite can be understood multi-dimensionally.

different districts, divisions, and regions of *Skilled Speakers International*. Beyond these events sanctioned by *Skilled Speakers International*, club members and guests saw each other socially. After every one hour and twenty-nine minute meeting, members and guests went out for post-meeting dinners. Invitations for social events in members' homes were often extended to club members and guests.

The *Indian Communicators Skilled Speakers Club* in the Silicon Valley, functioned the nearly the same way. Members and guests engaged in the same activity; they toasted to life, commented on current events, and spoke about their professional, public, and private lives in accordance to the guidelines of *Skilled Speakers International*. The only difference with this club was membership; there were twenty-paid *Indian Communicators Skilled Speakers Club* members, but only about twelve to fifteen attended meetings on a regular basis. Unlike the *Indian Professional Skilled Speakers Club* in Southern California, membership was an even mix of men and women, and many were married couples.

While guests were always welcome at both *Skilled Speakers Clubs*, full participation required membership. Guests were permitted to speak extemporaneously when called upon and observe the meetings, but were excluded from delivering prepared speeches, attending club business meetings, and participating events hosted by the wider organization. In order to maximize my observations and fully understand what it is like to be a member of both of these *Skilled Speakers International* clubs, I became a member (Wax 1980; Snow, Benford, and Anderson 1986; Hertz and Imber 1995; Hirsch 1995; and Loftland and Loftland 1995).

After obtaining consent from club members and human subjects approval through the University of California at Irvine, I engaged in complete participant observation for a total of three years in both research sites. This entailed doing everything that members did, from organizing and running meetings, holding several club offices, following the *Skilled Speakers International* curriculum, to even socializing with members. In the early stages of research, I fervently took notes on all aspects of the meetings and activities. My lengthy field notes included conversations among members and guests, verbatim quotes from their speeches and responses, and their overall behavior. As my contact with members extended to the telephone and over e-mail, I took notes on telephone conversations and saved all e-mail correspondence. I also documented my own activities, circumstances, and emotional responses to being a member of *Skilled Speakers International* because as Goodwin and Horowitz explain, "The 'I' is important to permit the reader to know where the researcher was at the time the data were collected and to explain the role the researcher played" (45). These notes document my subjective experiences in the field and explain how my role shaped the data that I observed and collected. This is addressed in detail in the second part of this chapter.

These research sites were conducive to note taking because members fulfilled roles during meetings that required them to take notes also. Note taking was a normal activity and members were well aware that I was studying them. As a result I produced rich field notes that captured the range of actors and perspective in the field. I became particularly interested in perspectives in action, or the naturally occurring conversations that occurred among and between club members and guests (Snow and Anderson 1993: 22; Morrill 1995: 15-16).

After meetings and events, I meticulously typed up my field notes in a chronological manner. I included my questions about events, members, and exchanges in the field as well as my analytical hunches. I would return to the field with these questions and analytical hunches in mind and interview members by comment (Snow, Zurcher, and Sjoberg 1982). This supplemental data gathering technique proved useful when verifying observations, broaching sensitive topics, assessing relationships, and obtaining clarification. I was quickly and unobtrusively able to get information in a timely manner and included it in my field notes.

As time progressed in the field and I began the process of open line-by-line coding. Asking broad questions like what is going on here generated numerous codes that I later organized into core themes. These themes included culture, status, people, scripts, professions, and gender, to name a few. With the help of *NVIVO*, a qualitative research software program, I re-coded the field notes using these themes and was able to generate short memos. My first memo was on gender norms in the field, particularly as they pertained to my role as a researcher and members' attitudes toward marriage. I wrote additional memos on how members displayed status and the mobility of their new second generation. This data shifted my research focus away from labor market discrimination to the construction of a culture of success. I rearticulated my research questions and took more pointed notes on these areas. In sum, I spent approximately three hundred hours in the field and nine hundred hours typing up field notes. This yielded nearly fifteen hundred pages of field notes, documents, and e-mails.

Despite this substantial informational yield, I could not fully answer the multifaceted research questions that this book investigates. In order to get at members' definitions of the culture of success, how they understood it, and its consequences, I needed to supplement my observations with interview data. While I strove to interview a complete sample of club members, I ended up interviewing active members only. This meant, members who attend weekly meeting and activities on a regular basis. I conducted in-depth interviews with twenty-two members of *Indian Professional Skilled Speakers International Club* in Southern California and fourteen members of the *Indian Communicators Skilled Speakers Club* in the Silicon Valley.

Data derived from complete participant observation informed the content of the interview instrument.[12] Study participant were asked a series of questions that were asked to elaborate on incidents and issues that took place in the field and also questions that were not directly observable. Early on I asked study participants standard questions about their background, migration experience, professional life, networks, *Skilled Speakers*, identity, and demographics. These questions were open-ended, semi-structured, and even unstructured.

However, as I logged and coded additional field notes, the interview instrument evolved according to preliminary findings. For example, after coding and writing a memo on gender norms in the field, I added questions on gender and club members' spouses to the interview instrument. The same is true of the mobility of the new second generation. The limited amount of data collected about the children of study participants in the field, led me to add addition questions about their children to the interview instrument. On occasion, interviews were conducted in two parts. I often asked members follow-up questions due to the length of time in the field and fact that they were interviewed over the span of two years. All interviews with members of *Skilled Speakers International* were audio-taped and all but two were transcribed verbatim.[13] I used *NVIVO*, a

---

[12] See Interview Instruments

[13] Background noise rendered two audio-tape recordings inaudible. I transcribed audible portions of these two interviews.

software program designed to assist in managing and coding qualitative data, to code the transcribed interviews according to core themes.

I also interviewed a comparison sample of eight Asian Indian elites who were not members of *Skilled Speakers International.* This comparison sample was a nonrandom sample. Using purposive and negative case sampling, I contacted fifteen Asian Indian elites who frequented the *Los Angeles Times, San Jose Mercury News,* and *India West* in person, by telephone, and via e-mail. I even attended dinner parties of wealthy acquaintances, cultural events, and charity benefits to network with this sub-sample and determine whether they held membership in *Skilled Speakers International.* Although approximately half contacted either me turned down or not respond to my e-mails or telephone calls, seven men and one woman agreed to be interviewed. In this sub-sample, ethnicity and elite status are held constant, and membership in *Skilled Speakers International* serves as the point of comparison. Four of these Asian Indian elite nonmembers resided in Southern California and the remaining four were from the Silicon Valley. All but one of the interviews were audio-taped and transcribed verbatim.[14] Interviewing a comparison sample mitigates against sampling bias. This also allows for claims to be made about generalizability. To what degree are members of *Skilled Speakers International* representative of Asian Indian elites?

This book, finally, relies on quantitative methods. Using data from the 2000 Integrated Public Use Microdata Series (IPUMS), I conducted crosstabulations to see if demographics are responsible for the divergent gender dynamics in the two research sites. Chapter four details that there is more to this story than demographics they and a case is made for qualitative inquiry.

Ultimately, answering the simple question of what is really going here is considerably complex. It takes complete participant observation, in-depth interviews, and quantitative data to adequately address. Even then, this overlooks a critical tool in documenting the culture of success among Asian Indian elites—the self or the researcher. While this

---

[14] After approaching the CEO of a major software company in the Silicon Valley at a charity event, he enthusiastically agreed to be interviewed, but asked that I complete it right at that moment. Unfortunately I did not have my tape recorder, but took notes during our forty-five minute un-taped interview.

section explored objective research methods, the next section details the more subjective aspects of my role as a researcher and how I curiously navigated the field.

THE SELF AS A RESEARCH TOOL AND GENDER RELATIONS IN THE FIELD

The previous section details the objective aspects of my research methods. However, it omits the problems and pitfalls that often plague qualitative researchers. Easterday, Papademas, Schorr, and Valentine (1977) remind social scientists that the subjective aspects of research are equally to address. They explain that, "Research courses and methodological texts only teach students how research ought to go, rather than how it does go in the real world. As social scientists, we have an obligation to share experiences with other researchers in order to develop our research skills and enterprise (Easterday et al 1977: 346)." Therefore, this section delves into how these rigorous and objective research procedures are impacted by subjective factors like my ethnicity, social status, age, and gender.

These subjective factors are critical to address in ethnographies because the "self," or the researcher, is a critical research tool (Powdermaker 1967; Golde 1970; Nader 1970, 1975; Johnson 1975; Warren and Rasmussen 1977; Goodwin and Horowitz 2002). Surprisingly, this is often overlooked in scholarship on research methods, despite ethnographers arguing that how they capture the cultures that they study involves much more than just objective research methods.[15] Equally important is their own ability to empathize with others and the capacity to capture the inner feelings of the people that they study. This being the case, they stress that those who engage in this method should record the process of interacting with the people that they study and, more specifically, monitor how their own characteristics enable and constrain data access and collection.[16]

---

[15] Goodwin and Horowitz (2002) explain that prior to the 1960s, books published in sociology rarely included methodological appendices.

[16] Powdermaker (1967: 9) explains that, "A scientific discussion of field work method should include considerable detail about the observer: the role he plays, his personality, and other relevant facts concerning his position and functioning in the society studied."

Ethnicity, social status, age, and gender are four such characteristics that enabled and constrained data collection in this study. In the following sections, I detail the complexities of conducting fieldwork, perhaps more appropriately described as "homework,"[17] within my own community. While sharing the ethnic background of my study participants was a passport into the research sites and a merit to approach the comparison group, my social status, age, and gender frequently rendered me an outsider. This, however, did not necessarily constrain access to data; sometimes being an outsider enables data access and collection.

Beyond the Insider and Outsider Perspective

While most assume that researchers are regarded as insiders when studying coethnics, this is not the case. Presenting researchers as insiders or outsiders is actually a false dichotomy; the relationship between researchers and the groups that they study is far more complex and multilayered (Golde 1970; Stack 1974; Zinn 1979; Visweswaran 1994; Manalansan 2000; Vo 2000). Ethnographic research does not follow the linear path of an outsider eventually becoming an insider; it, instead, follows the logic of normal human exchange and therefore includes chance happenings, frustrations and rewards, unsought insights, stumbled upon understandings, and never resolved misunderstandings (Golde 1970: 3). In ethnographic research being an insider and outsider is negotiated on a continual basis.

Indeed, I share an ethnic identity with my study participants; we all ethnically identified as Asian Indian in some respect. This enables access to the research site as both clubs cater to Asian Indian professionals. Hence, as prior noted, my fieldwork is "homework" in the sense that I study my own society at home (Visweswaran 1994; Manalansan 2000; Vo 2000). For example, my Asian Indian ethnicity fosters trust with study participants and wider access to their private social worlds that a non-Asian Indian researcher may not have experienced (Manalansan 2000). Moreover, chapters four and five of

---

[17] Visweswaran (1994) cleverly refers to conducting research in one's own community as homework. She argues that this term appropriately decolonizes ethnographies and highlights how coethnic researchers and subjects are linked in complicated ways.

this book are a direct result of my status as an insider along ethnic lines. Members quickly invited me into their homes for Asian Indian social gatherings. Here I met their spouses, children, extended family, and friends and gathered data on how personal success is negotiated through the family.

Additionally, many members assumed that I understood and practiced Asian Indian cultural norms and held me to them. For instance, early into my research, *Arvind's* wife's brother died in a tragic car accident in India. Although I hardly knew the club members, they assumed that I would go with them to *Arvind's* home and offer condolences. Therefore, being an ethnic insider accelerated the process of establishing rapport; I had access to the private lives of these Asian Indian professionals early into the study.

However, a significant difference between them and myself is status—at the time that I conducted my research I was a graduate student in sociology. While hard to believe, this is remarkably different from being an elite. There are some status markers that are beyond the reach of a graduate student like myself. Study participants frequently arrived at weekly meetings and events in their luxury automobiles after jet setting across the globe in first class travel. However, I did so in my Volkswagen Golf after teaching course discussion sections at the University of California at Irvine. Members in the *Indian Professional Skilled Speakers Club* adhered to a professional dress code that allowed entry into the usually closed fine dining establishments frequented post meetings.[18] Although I made sure to dress the part of a professional, one member remarked that my car was not up to professional par.

As club members lingered in the *Southland* Public library parking lot, *Kavi*, the club epicurean, announced the venue for the post meeting dinner—*Arte Café*—a local French restaurant. While making our way to each of our cars, *Vik* jingled his keys in my direction and said, "Here, drive my S-Class to the restaurant. Your car just doesn't fit you." I glibly responded with, "Hey, what do you have against Volkswagens? Aren't they also German engineered? I like my car. It gets me where I need to go." *Vik* then replied, "Oh, that's a good quality—being self-made—but come by my house and I'll swap your Golf with one of our BMWs or a Lexus. You should be driving a car like that." Rather than

---

[18] *Kavi,* the club epicurean, had arrangements with several local restaurateurs to remain open late to serve members of the *Indian Professional Skilled Speakers Club.*

taking offense to this exchange, I focus on its analytic merit. Exchanges like this highlight that one can simultaneously occupy the status of an insider and outsider. I am an insider because I am of Asian Indian ethnicity, am an accepted club member, and am on my way to being a professional, albeit in a nontraditional sense. On the other hand, I am an outsider because of my lower social status as a middle class graduate student.

Being an insider and outsider constrains and enables research. For example, being an outsider in terms of social class and status enables research in the sense that it elicits comparison by members. *Vik's* comment about my unfitting car marks how he understands difference and is illustrative of the material status symbols common among Asian Indian elites in Southern California. A researcher from the same social class and status might miss this seemingly obvious finding, making insider social status a constraint on research.

That club members explained their activities in great detail because of my status as a graduate student, also enabled research. When I casually asked *Vik* how his day was, he explained that he had just come from a meeting with the CEO of Starbucks who was interested in expanding the chain to India. *Vik* slowly broke down the business decisions involved in such a venture and patiently addressed my questions. Most club members, like *Vik*, shared their day-to-day experiences with great candor. Much of this had to do with my lower social status as a graduate student and their interest in facilitating my research.

On three occasions, however, my lower social status as a graduate student constrained my research. Interestingly these challenging exchanges occurred with members of the comparison sample. While I had sustained contact and significant rapport with club members, my exposure to Asian Indian elites in the comparison sample was limited to one or two encounters. As a result, they seemed less obliged to participate in the study by granting me an interview. These three challenging exchanges occurred with elites of the Southern California comparison sample. These three Asian Indian elites graced the *Los Angeles Times* on a number of occasions and despite meeting me at a charity dinner, fundraising event for a prominent politician, and an Asian Indian culture show, they had no recollection of doing so. Three e-mails and two phone calls later, two of these Asian Indian elites agreed to be interviewed. However the terms of the interview were, "don't call us, we will call you." And their secretaries eventually did. This reminded me of my low social status as a graduate student. Although I acquired my own social and cultural capital in the process of studying exactly that among Asian Indian elites, on these occasions it was not enough to schedule an interview with one attempt.

On another occasion, I approached *Ashwin,* a popular Asian Indian community figure with aspirations for a career in mainstream politics. I introduced myself as a doctoral candidate and explained that my famous advisor suggested that I contact him for an interview. The flattery worked and I was granted an interview. When I arrived at his office and informed his secretary that I was here for our 10:00 am meeting, she buzzed his office and had me take a seat. Portly *Ashwin* tottered his way down the hallway and extended his hand. With my high heels on, I towered over the five feet two inches man, but he made himself seem bigger as he coolly asked, "I thought your professor was coming also...?" At first I was a little shocked and was tempted to remind him that I am a doctoral candidate and scholar, but instead I replied, "Oh, I do the interviews. My professor helps more when I take the data apart and actually write." He then replied, "Oh, of course. He's probably really busy as a professor." While on a human level this exchange is insulting, as a researcher it is display of social status that is an empirical finding. In our exchange *Ashwin* signals our status difference to his watchful staff. He is too important to be interviewed by an outsider—a low status graduate student. Moreover, it seems that he was looking for personal gain from the interview in the form of networking with a famous professor. His calculation is telling of how social networks are exploited for personal mobility and, in this specific case, in the political sphere. This exchange also underscores the rules of reciprocity in social research and that data access is a constant negotiation that is hardly free.[19]

---

[19] In the research setting, reciprocity refers to repaying study participants for the data that they provide. Golde (1970: 83) and Nader (1970: 101) assert that some form of reciprocity is necessary in fieldwork. Reciprocity enhances rapport by easing acceptance and reducing conflict. Most study participants were flattered that I wanted to interview them and a simple thank you card sufficed. However, a few participants wanted greater returns for an interview. This is elaborated in the following section on the impact of gender on data access and collection.

My age is another personal characteristic that is noticeably different from study participants; the majority of them are significantly older than me. I spent my mid-to-late twenties in the field and, similar to my lower social status, this also often facilitated data access and collection. As prior mentioned, most study participants viewed me as self-made, although far from the truth, and proactive. They appreciated these perceived qualities and, for the most part, wanted to help me with my study.

My age often elicited conversations about study participants' own children. For example, although I had met *Gary's* wife, he never let on that he had a daughter during club meetings or post meeting dinners. One cold evening, I attended a club meeting out of professional dress code wearing jeans, tennis shoes, a sweatshirt, and my hair in a ponytail. *Gary* was the usually the first club member to point out of violations of club decorum, but instead of scolding me for my unprofessional appearance, he said, "I've never seen you look so casual. When you wear your hair like that, you remind me of my daughter. She's not like you—she is a tomboy." This conversation allowed me to interview *Gary* by comment about his daughter. I tried to probe further, but when I inquired about her education and occupation *Gary* changed the subject and then walked away. His surprising reaction perked my curiosity about the children of Asian Indian elites. These types of conversations and meetings fueled chapter five, which explores the prospects of mobility for the children of Asian Indian elites. It seems that my relative youth allowed for the exploration of the children of Asian Indian elites in this book.

Other instances shed light on how Asian Indian elites interact with their children. During an interview over *dim sum* with *Dr. Batra* and his ten-year-old daughter, *Sonia,* he turned to her and scolded her about her poor posture at the dinner table. In frustration, he asked if I would keep her for the weekend and turn her into a proper young lady. He vented about how *Sonia* needed a suitable role model in life. She rolled her eyes and said, "My dad likes you." This exchange sheds light on the culture of success as it pertains to the children of Asian Indian elites and also addresses the role that gender plays in the field.

The Impact of Gender on Data Access and Collection

Golde (1970: 3) remarks that in most non-literate cultures being visited by a woman who engages in activities outside the scope of typical women's roles is unusual. However, the same is true of highly literate cultures like that of Asian Indian elites in the United States. As advanced later in chapter three, a common perception among club members in Southern California is that Asian Indian women have little need for communication and leadership skills. This made my presence in the club and unusual event and contrary to their perception of roles appropriate for women. But as Geer (1977: 345) explains, this worked to my advantage:

> The most handicapped observer is the one doing people and situations he/she is closest to. Hence, women are in luck in a male-run world. They can see how few clothes the emperor has on, question the accepted, what is taken for granted.

After just one hour in the field, I started to receive romantically inclined e-mails and telephone calls from club members. Having introduced myself as a sociologist who studies the immigration of the highly skilled, led other members to e-mail and call with inquiries about my research. Two members divulged that they had conducted an Internet search of my name and read a paper that I had written which was posted online. Despite concerns of social desirability bias, I had never come across a more willing sample of study participants; they wanted to talk to me.

To a large degree, my gender enabled data access and collection in the Southern California research site. In this competitive and nearly exclusive male environment, most male Asian Indian elites found me unthreatening. As later addressed in chapter four, the few women that entered the male realm of the *Indian Professional Skilled Speakers Club* were viewed in terms of traditional Indian gender roles, as was I.[20] Most male members, like *Gary,* regarded them as someone's wife, sibling, or daughter, and not competition:

> Off and on we get women, but for the most part it is men. Indian women…the girls…the different ethnic backgrounds from back in Indian…number one, I don't think based on the

---

[20] Lee's (2002: 219-226) experience is similar. As she collected data for her study on merchant-customer relations in New York and Philadelphia, study participants viewed her according to the gender roles of either a daughter or a sex object.

types of jobs they do, they don't need *Skilled Speakers* in a big way. As many Indian people as there are here, it is still a closed community. Suppose you go and you stutter and are not able to communicate and someone is there that knows your brother or friend—that might make fun of you. Men sort of get away with it, but girls are still shy and affected more. Some girls have a fear complex. Also their criticism probably won't be taken seriously because they are seen as someone's daughter or sister.

Gary's understanding of the appropriate roles of women in the Indian community sheds light on the male power structure of the *Indian Professional Skilled Speakers Club*. Many male members shared in Gary's sentiment—women lower the rigor of the club. Therefore this perception of women as periphery members also extended to my role as a researcher.

This is in line with the scholarship on sex and gender in field research (Golde 1970; Johnson 1975; Kanter 1975; Warren and Rasmussen 1977). Women are perceived as sexually provocative, especially when unmarried. Warren and Rasmussen argue that this has two effects: (1) it eases access to information from men; and (2) is threatening to other women (1977: 352). The ease of information from men is clearly evident in the interview process. While I was not regarded as direct competition to them, they competed with each other for my attention. *Anisha* explains,

> You are hands down the hottest thing to walk through our doors. Between *Devan, Vik, Karsh,* and *Nikhil* it is just competition now. That's just a lot of testosterone and when one girl shows up, it really sort of tugs in all sorts of directions. Who is going to ask her out first? Who's got dibs on her? It is the, "I saw her first" type thing. Who can sweet-talk her into a date? They are friends, yet they have this competitive relationship too.

This competition among single male members helped with my collection of data. Despite their personal motives, I had a sample of willing study participants.

As addressed earlier, a formidable obstacle to studying up is that elite study participants are often very busy. In my prior research (Sandhu 2002) as well as with the comparison sample in this study, scheduling in-depth interviews were rather challenging. Often times this meant compromising on methods by being flexible about alternative interview modes. I literally chased after study participants and conducted interviews at their convenience, even if that meant waiting while they attended to business, traveling with them on their way to meetings, conducting the interview in parts on the telephone, or going running with them with my tape-recorder in hand. Despite these inconsistencies in interview modes, how these interviews were completed revealed additional facets of the lives of these busy immigrant professionals.

In this ethnographic study however, scheduling interviews with club members was not a problem at all.[21] Many male members contacted me and scheduled interviews on their own. For example, *Vik,* a thirty-five year old president of a global aviation company, was eager to help me with my research. As I suggested venues for the interview like my office or a coffee shop, he insisted that the interview be conducted over dinner. I agreed, as I felt obliged to study participants that gave so much of their time for my study. However, I had no idea that dinner would entail a boat ride and tour of the local harbor. After asking all of my interview questions, *Vik* remarked that agreeing to an interview was the only way that he could spend time with me. I felt like I was dating for data and was initially concerned about social desirability bias. However, every interaction is data to a researcher and this was no different. Understanding that my gender role, even as a researcher, was framed by gender norms in the *Indian Professional Skilled Speakers Club* made even this experience illustrative of just that—the norms of the club. Their regard of me was the same as any other young, unmarried woman in the club—a periphery member with the potential of a romantic partner.

I asked *Dr. Batra* for an interview and he happily obliged. In addition to being a professor at a prestigious medical school in Southern California, he is the creator and patent holder of a lifesaving medication. On a Thursday evening I received an e-mail from *Dr.*

---

[21] However, conducting the interviews are an entirely different story. In a later section, I will address the fine line between retaining self-respect and maintaining established rapport with study participants.

Batra with a request regarding the interview: he was staying at the Ritz Carlton in Marina del Rey and suggested that I come to his hotel on Friday evening for dinner and then we could complete the interview. While he may have suggested Friday night at his hotel because he is a busy doctor and was fitting me into his schedule, it seemed rather inappropriate. I responded diplomatically: "I hear that they have a great Sunday Brunch at the Ritz. Enjoy your stay. How about we meet another time?"

We later scheduled an interview at a closer site and over *dim sum*. *Dr. Batra's* ten-year-old daughter was present. However after the interview, he insisted that I go on a walk with them. While I did not feel inclined, I felt obliged because he had just completed the interview and conducting interviews according to study participants' terms served functioned as reciprocity. Also, because encounters with club members occurred on a regular basis, I had to maintain a civil relationship with them. However, this daytime interview had progressed into the early evening and I finally disengaged by explaining that I had to return to Irvine.

Situations like these capture the tension between being human and our jobs as researchers. On one hand an emergent empirical finding is exciting and are fuel for this book. On a human level, however, situations like these are confusing and can be demoralizing. Nader (1970: 111) argues that this is the nature of ethnographic research:

> The personal aspects of field work necessarily involve feelings
> of ambivalence — simultaneous feelings of attraction and
> repulsion. These feelings may be directed toward the people
> one is studying, toward oneself, and toward the state of the
> profession.

My field notes document this ambivalence between human reactions and empirical findings. For example, at a club contest, *Nikhil* delivered following inappropriate introduction of me: "If this hot member were a traffic sign, she would be danger curves ahead." I quipped back, "I think he must referring to my spontaneous personality," which made the audience laugh. Comments like these were common throughout my time in the field and reminded me of the 1980s sexual harassment public service announcement put out by the American Women in Radio and Television Incorporation. In their thirty-second clip, a male employer makes inappropriate comments to a woman subordinate. With every inappropriate comment, she shrinks. Finally, she returns to her normal size and retorts, "No, this is sexual harassment and I'm not going to take it." While I shrunk as a woman, I grew as a researcher. After all, sexual harassment is data, I took it, and I wrote about it.

On three occasions, study participants went a bit too far and compromised my access to data.[22] All three incidents occurred with unmarried male members. One was in his early thirties, while the other two were in their early forties. To prevent overraport and fact check, I made sure to equalize time with all people in the field (Easterday et al 1977; Loftland et al 2006).[23] I would try to sit by a different member at each meeting, post meeting dinners, and club events. I used these opportunities to interview members by comment.

I conversed with *Karsh*, one of the younger club members, about his position in the organization. I specifically inquired about the interaction between first and second generation immigrants in the club. He expressed bitterness toward first generation immigrants and disliked their tendency to parent younger people. He served as an excellent source for information on the children of club members as he socialized with many of them. I conducted an informational telephone interview with him in the early stages of research.

In our less formal exchanges, he frequently discussed the Asian Indian marriage market and how he was a hot commodity on it: "I mean, how many Indian guys do you know that look like me? Everywhere I go, girls are all over me." Then, on our way to a banquet committee meeting, *Karsh* explained that his parents were pressuring him to get married. He was so irritated that he stopped communicating with them for several months. He then said, "Hey, we'd be good together. We should go out." I explained that while he was a nice person, it would not be a good idea since I was studying the club and its members, including him. I added that I was there on behalf of my

---

[22] While Johnson (1975) argues that the significance of sexual attractiveness in work settings is more muted and less overt than the sex industry, perhaps this study reveals that this is not necessarily the case.

[23] Golde (1970: 85-86) cautions against overrapport or intimate involvements with study participants. This can curtail a researcher's objectivity. In addition, it is difficult to predict the short and long term repercussions of such relations.

university and needed to behave professionally and appropriately. In this case, maintaining access, particularly after turning down a romantic proposition, made my gender a constraint. *Karsh* stopped interacting with me in the field and when I later asked to interview him, he bitterly declined. I took his cryptic e-mail as a no: "Sabeen, I talk to myself out loud in the third person. Do you need to know more than that?"

At a post meeting dinner, tempers flared when *Nikhil* found out that I was conducting my a study on the club. While all other members consented and received a copy of the human subjects agreement, *Nikhil* recently returned to the club after a two-year hiatus and had not yet been informed. *Nikhil* angrily inquired, "What does that mean—you're doing a study on the club?" I explained the premise of my project and my research methods. I assured him of confidentiality and reminded him of the dearth of literature on Asian Indians. However, his concerns boiled down to one issue—"does this mean we can't have a relationship?" Surprised by his reaction, I replied, "*Nikhil,* we don't have a relationship so why are you concerned?" Vexed, he slammed glass on the dinner table and said, "Keep my name out of your study." I agreed to do so. However as time progressed, *Nikhil* seemed to feel left out of the research process and said that it was okay to include him in the study. He asked me to interview him, but listed a few conditions: (1) I would attend the premiere of a Hollywood film with him; and (2) be open to a romantic relationship with him. This time my patience was vexed and I turned him down. *Nikhil* and I interacted on a frequent basis via e-mail and telephone. He also took center stage at club meetings and because he later agreed to be included in the study, I had sufficient data on him. While I missed the opportunity to interview *Nikhil,* my stance sent a message to other study participants—I was serious scholar who would not be harassed and manipulated. I would not date for data. I was there for the purpose of research, not romance. After word got around about my encounter with *Nikhil,* three members remarked on my professionalism, apologized for *Nikhil's* behavior, and lauded my no-dating stance.[24]

---

[24] Curiously, one of these three members suggested that I conduct my interview with him on his way to New York. He said, "I'll fly you there, we can have dinner, catch a show, you can do your interview, and I'll bring you right back." I explained that I had a lot of homework and suggested an alternative venue for the interview—a local Starbucks.

However, one member did not get the message and went to great lengths, four hundred miles, to pursue me or experience another *Skilled Speakers Club*. During my three years of fieldwork, I spent the school term in Southern California and the summers in the Silicon Valley. When I departed Southern California in June of 2005, *Saif*, a forty-year-old electrical engineer, inquired about my plans for the summer. In jest, I told him that I was "two-timing" the *Indian Professional Skilled Speakers Club*. I innocently shared that my study included another site in the Silicon Valley that was also a club for Indian professionals. He said that he would miss me over the summer and then we parted ways, or so I thought. To my surprise, *Saif* showed up at a Thursday night meeting of the *Indian Communicators Skilled Speakers Club* in the Silicon Valley. I wondered what he was doing here and felt uneasy because my two research sites were colliding. *Saif* explained that he looked the club up on the Internet, but was really hungry and asked if I wanted to go out to dinner with him instead. I explained that I could not as I had a role to fulfill during the meeting. He ended up staying for the meeting and waited to speak to me at its close.

Although I had already interviewed him in Southern California, I knew that I would encounter him in the field again. This is one of the challenges of sustained contact with study participants. While the benefits of prolonged fieldwork out weight its costs, managing my role as a researcher twenty-four hours a day and for several years was taxing. While I felt obliged to speak to him, I did not want to have dinner with him or anything more. So, I expressed a sense of urgency and said, "*Saif*, it was so nice seeing you. I hope that you enjoy your stay here. I'll see you in Southern California in September." When September arrived, neither of us acknowledged his trip to the *Indian Communicators Club in the Silicon Valley*. I invoked my researcher role. I no longer needed interview data from him, so I had no sociological reason to have dinner with him.

In the Silicon Valley I encountered comparatively less researcher dilemmas as a result of my gender. In fact only one instance appears in my field notes. It was during an open house event that the club hosted to increase membership. I was in the midst of a conversation with the president of the club when a forty-something, Asian Indian man, wearing jeans, a polo shirt, and evidence of a few too many alcoholic beverages approached us. I assumed that he had business with the club president because she turned to him and said, "Hello, how are you?

Did you need to speak with me?" To my surprise he pointed in my direction and said, "No, I am waiting to talk to her." I was expressionless as the president replied, "Who isn't," and laughed. I introduced myself and asked him what I could help him with. He said, "I want to know about this outfit. Where did you get it?" I told him that I bought it where most people buy clothes—the shopping mall. I then excused myself, but he followed me and announced to his entourage, "This beautiful girl is stalking me." They seemed embarrassed of his behavior and motioned for him to leave me alone.

This incident occurred with a guest at an event open to the public. However, there were no instances of inappropriate behavior or even comments directed at the opposite gender in the *Indian Communicators Skilled Speakers Club* in the Silicon Valley. This may largely be a result of the gender makeup of the club; membership was an even mix of men and women and they were all married. Some women, however, remarked upon the fact that I was unmarried. As addressed earlier, women are often perceived as sexually provocative, especially when unmarried. While this eases access to information from men, other women tend to see them as a threat (Golde 1970; Warren and Rasmussen 1977).

Prior to the start of the meeting, *Saira* asked whether I would drive her to a division competition scheduled for later that week. The division competition was to take place at a large software company in the Silicon Valley and it seemed sensible to carpool. *Zaiden,* a male member, overheard us and asked if I would mind picking him up as well since it was on my way. I agreed and we all showed up at the competition together. During the dinner the break, *Samantha* and *Arleen* approached me and asked how far my house was from *Zaiden's* office. I explained that his office was on my to *Saira's* house, who I had picked up as well. *Samantha* explained her concern: "Oh, you're a young, unmarried girl. We would have picked him up. Next time, don't give him a ride." Despite our carpool including *Saira, Samantha* and *Arleen's* concerns illustrate what is defined as appropriate behavior for unmarried women in the club.

This interaction illustrates the attitudes and mechanisms of social control prevalent in the *Indian Communicators Skilled Speakers Club* and even wider Asian Indian community. Apparently carpooling with a married man is viewed as suspect and I was quickly warned. In some respects, *Samantha* and *Arleen* were trying to protect me or urge me to conform to the norms of the club and culture.[25] Nevertheless, in this research site, both male and female members were equally intent on helping me with my project. Despite these two incidents, I did not feel the same degree of harassment as encountered in the *Indian Professional Skilled Speakers Club* in Southern California.

While many of my academic colleagues expressed concern over issues of overrapport, going native, and social desirability bias in my study, I reminded them of three objective facts: (1) interviews are not sole source data in this study; (2) the sheer length of time in the field fosters data triangulation; and (3) these subjective encounters also constitute empirical data that are indicative of the cultural norms and power structure in the organization and the wider Asian Indian community. Furthermore, over the course of three years in the field, I was adequately able to fact check.[26] I had open access to the work, public, and private worlds of these members where I compared what they said to what they actually did. The sheer magnitude of empirical data allays concerns of overrapport, going native, and social desirability bias. After all, my interaction with Asian Indian elites in both research sites and the comparison sample is the basis for the three empirical chapters at the heart of this book.

This chapter detailed the methodological rigors of ethnographic research. As addressed above, qualitative researchers face methodological issues and must make choices at every stage of the research process to answer new research questions, manage unanticipated concerns, and maintain rapport with study participants (Goodwin and Horowitz 2002). Despite having a solid methodological plan for researching and writing a book on Asian Indian elites, ethnographic research reflects the surprises of social life. Perhaps Nader captures it best: "Field work is a series of trials and errors.

---

[25] Golde explains that these types of interactions are actually warnings veiled as protective measures. They are telling of the attitudes and mechanisms of social control in communities and organizations. Golde elaborates that, "Once in the field, gossip, and rumors, insinuations of wrongdoing, overt and disguised sexual encounters initiated by men, and active attempts to control and limit the woman's freedom of movement are further expressions of this attitude" (1970: 6).

[26] Morrill and Fine (1997:443) note that the length of time spent in the field often improves the quality of research. As researchers spend more time in the field, observations become more intense and they gain a familiarity and understanding of a, once unfamiliar, research situation.

When one makes a daring stab at building rapport and is successful, the experience is exhilarating"(1970: 101). The next three empirical chapters are the exhilarating products of my objective research procedures and how I navigated opportunities and constraints in the field.

CHAPTER THREE

Constructing a Culture of Success

"The first question God is going to ask us when we die and meet him or her is what did you do with all the time and the gifts I gave you. I am just collecting answers to give to God."

--Rahul, 43 year-old Certified Public Accountant, Venture Capitalist, and Philanthropist

Although no scholarly study to date has focused on *Skilled Speakers International*, study participants were accustomed to being interviewed about their labor market success and global philanthropy by other scholars and the mainstream and coethnic media. For example, I scheduled an interview with *Vijay*, an angel investor in the Silicon Valley. His secretary had me take a seat in the waiting area outside of his office. To while away the time, I looked over my interview instrument, but overheard him talking to someone about me. *Vijay* said, "Oh, there she is," and proceeded to introduce me to an economics professor from Stanford University. He playfully said, "Here's your future competition," and explained that the economics professor from Stanford had just interviewed him for a similar study.

Although we were interrupted during the interview because he needed to answer another angel investor's burning question about a suitable wine pairing for grilled salmon, *Vijay* answered every question I asked with finesse. He brought up his close relationship with former president Bill Clinton several times and even shared that he beat him at a game of golf. When I asked him how he became so successful, he cited the Roman philosopher, Lucius Annaeus Seneca: "Luck is where preparation meets opportunity." However, when my queries became more personal this articulate angel investor took some long pauses and delivered unscripted answers about his wife's role in his work and the prospects of his children's mobility.[27] After concluding the interview, *Vijay* handed me a recently published book about entrepreneurs in the Silicon Valley and explained that he was featured in it. As I later read the chapter on him, I realized that he is asked about his success so often that he has an answer down to a script.

This was the case with the majority of study participants; they often provided me with additional sources of data that documented their success, like media coverage. For example, prior to our interview, *Rahul* e-mailed me three newspaper articles that highlighted his achievements. Interestingly, when I asked how he became so successful, his response was exactly what he was quoted as stating in all three articles: "The first question God is going to ask us when we die and meet him or her is what did you do with all the time and the gifts I gave you. I am just collecting answers to give to God."

As addressed in the prior chapter on research methods, Thomas (1995) notes that elites have a three-fold persona: individual, position, and organizational. If solely relying on interview data, the researcher must separate each persona. One way to do this is through participant observation because elites can then be understood multi-dimensionally. Moreover, observing them over an extended period of time builds rapport and may disarm them from formal corporate scripts and prepared public relations responses. And, indeed, complete participant observation lends itself to this. However, noting Morrill's (1995: 14-16) remarks about scripts warrants an examination of the meaning and function of them. Morrill argues that one of the ways that culture becomes visible and expressed is through schemas, scripts, and stories. Morrill elaborates that schemas, scripts, and stories convey structure and context to individuals. They also are cultural tools that signal appropriate roles, shape actions, and ultimately construct meaning.

Therefore, a way to uncover how Asian Indian elites understand their own success and achievements is to examine their schemas, formal scripts, and stories about success. This chapter examines precisely this; how is the culture of success constructed and what are its consequences for Asian Indian elites? Based on data from complete participant observation and forty-four in-depth interviews, Asian Indian

---

[27] These issues are the focus of chapters four and five of this book.

elites define and understand their success in direct contrast to the perceptions and stereotypes that are assigned to the wider Asian Indian population in the United States. They see their own success as atypical. In their scripts, they forward that they are a different kind of smart, have different kinds of social and cultural capital, and engage in a different kind of assimilation. In addition to this distancing or "othering" from the wider population of Asian Indians, these trends contradict what classic models of assimilation posit—do first generation immigrants only accommodate to life in the United States (Park and Burgess 1921; Gordon 1964; Shibutani and Kwan 1965; Gans 1973; Glazer and Moynihan 1970)? This case uncovers a new path of assimilation among first generation Asian Indian elites in Southern California and the Silicon Valley—active assimilation.[28]

As addressed in the introduction of this book, scholars (Gans 1979, 1992; Nagel 1996; Waters 1999; Brubaker 2001; Portes and Rumbaut 2001; Rumbaut 2002, 2011; Alba and Nee 2003; Cornell and Hartmann 2007) have critiqued the assumptions embedded in classic models of assimilation. To elaborate, classic models of assimilation have earned a bad name in the social sciences for positing a unidirectional process of eventual Anglo conformity. As a result, assimilation as a theory applied to post 1965 immigrants was dubbed politically disreputable and was analytically discredited.

Nevertheless, it is important to note that processes of change do occur when immigrants negotiate host societies. Scholars (Waters 1999; Foner et al 2000) posit that this begins even before the demographic process of migration, often in the sending country. Therefore assimilation as a concept, not as a theory, remains relevant. In this study I use assimilation as a context bound concept that helps explain the changes that Asian Indian elites, their spouses, and children negotiate in Southern California and the Silicon Valley. A key critique

---

[28] Park and Burgess (1921) argue that all ethnic groups experience four basic processes of social interaction: (1) competition; (2) conflict; (3) accommodation; and (4) assimilation. They distinguish between accommodation and assimilation: ethnic groups are conscious of accommodation, which takes place quickly, while assimilation occurs unconsciously and is more subtle and gradual. They further argue that accommodation is the modal process of first generation immigrants, while assimilation is reserved for the second generation (Rumbaut 1999: 186; 2011: 196).

of assimilation theories is the question of what immigrants are assimilating to. For example, what exactly constitutes mainstream culture today? Strategically, in this study Asian Indian elites are assimilating in suburban neighborhoods nestled in majority minority regions of the United States (Southern California and the Silicon Valley). They are also actively assimilating to corporate culture which remains largely upper class and white.[29]

A DIFFERENT KIND OF SMART

When asked to list common stereotypes about Asian Indians, the majority of study participants amusingly reported a curious array: Asian Indians are bad drivers, they are good at yoga, they speak with heavy and unattractive accents, they are doctors, lawyers, and engineers, they ride magic carpets and camels, and are smart. This question often elicited laughter among study participants. When I asked whether they had personally encountered any of these stereotypes or whether they applied to them, all study participants expressed that being stereotyped as smart had some truth to it and often worked to their benefit. For example, *Paul*, a thirty-one-year old internist, embraces the stereotype of Asian Indians being good doctors:

> It definitely plays a role in regards to reputation. Um…because there are a lot of patients who say, "Oh, Indians are good doctors." I hear that every week. I think that's fine. It is better than Indians are bad doctors. So I don't mind that at all. I think it is a good stereotype. And it is a stereotype, but it is a stereotype that plays in my favor. My supervisors— I don't necessarily think that they see me as a better doctor because I'm Indian, but in general I think the stereotype is a good thing.

Just as *Paul* gains credibility as a doctor because he is Asian Indian, *Vikas*, a twenty-six-year-old chief technology officer of a now failed

---

[29]Despite the visibility of Asian Indians in the fields of technology, medicine, and even politics, a recent report published on March 20th, 2012 by the Leadership Education for Asian Pacifics documents that they represent only 2.4 percent of the boards of directors of Fortune 500 companies (Springer 2012).

start-up, does so in the information technology sector. *Vikas* explains the benefits of positive stereotyping:

> I know this from being an entrepreneur (laughs) but when venture capitalists see an Indian CTO, they boost your points in their mind. Their perception of you goes up. It is based on a string of highly successful startups in the Silicon Valley that have started from absolute moguls that came from India and have been tremendously successful in the past couple of decades. So there's that precedent for Indians to be very successful. They see a tech boom happening in India and they see Indians starting with nothing, being a Third World Country and creating software that rivals the world's best. So they have respect for us now and they don't really need to know you, they just assume. They label you as such—a success.

Paul and *Vikas*, two second-generation Asian Indians, enjoy being labeled successes. This label comes with perceived benefits: *Paul's* patients have greater faith in his medical opinions and *Vikas* commands venture capital by virtue of his ethnicity.

Like *Paul* and *Vikas*, *Dr.* Pilla takes pride in the success of fellow Asian Indians and their second generation:

> One good thing about this country is that they respect merit. All the Indians that came before us made a really good impression. If you go to high schools, the kids that are smart are the Indians. If you go to math departments and the spelling bees, I have one thing to say—Indian kids, Indian kids, and Indian kids. Maybe the parental support and family environment and the effort. I guess we make them special and they know that. Very few Indian kids are bad or don't perform well. So if you actually don't do well it is a surprise. You are Indian and don't know…?

However, when I asked *Dr. Pilla* whether Asian Indians are positively stereotyped in the United States, he disagreed. He forcefully replied, "No, Indians have earned it." He then added that it is difficult for Americans to compete with Asian Indians and their children because they are brought up to excel. *Dr. Pilla* argued that success for Asian Indians elites and their next generation is a given and comes with relative ease.

While one would think that Asian Indian elites face the challenge of living up to such labels, the opposite is true. They, instead, face the challenge of being exceptions to these labels. They argue that these labels are merely applicable to the wider Asian Indian community and, as elites, they see themselves as atypical Asian Indians. They define their success in terms of how they exceed or are exceptions to common stereotypes like being smart, culturally intransigent, or poor communicators. When they display behaviors and articulate scripts in direct contrast to these stereotypes, they are constructing and defining the culture of success for Asian Indian elites. It seems that Asian Indian elites are borrowing the cultural standards of native-born white Americans and drawing moral, socioeconomic, and cultural boundaries against other Asian Indians (Lamont 1992). Unlike them, Asian Indian elites have more than just technical smarts, have actively assimilated to American culture, and have excellent communication and leadership skills.

Different from *Paul, Vikas*, and *Dr. Pilla,* the majority most study participants expressed that their smarts are beyond being book smart and having technical competence. As Asian Indian elites, they are well rounded, street smart, and highly sociable. *Ana,* a twenty-six-year-old financial analyst explains,

> I think we're very lucky because we have very good stereotypes that we're hardworking, the educational background, the family values, everything like that so I think I fit the mold. I fit the stereotype. I don't want to be caught in the… well let's see… what are the right words…? You know, that you are not social and you are more book smart than street smart. Maybe there are some and you get certain engineers, but again it's your own personality and who you are. I think that every stereotype that I have sort of heard has been a good one.

Ana further elaborates that being Asian Indian seems to work to her advantage in the financial industry. She stood out as the only Asian Indian in a group of fifteen analysts and noted that her supervisors and coworkers automatically thought that she was smart. She explains, "It helps to have that on your side when you are working with two million dollars or more in investable assets. You want to come across as someone capable of running analytics." Despite the perceived benefits from being stereotyped as smart, *Ana* highlights the potential downside—being stereotyped as socially inept and associates it with the engineering profession.

This stereotype is widespread and well documented in empirical studies as well as federal reports on glass ceilings (Fernandez 1998; Woo 2000; Prashad 2000; Varma 2006). For example, Varma's (2006: 62-69) study on Asian Indian engineers in the United States documents that Asian Indians are commonly viewed as economic people. This is because the widespread belief is that they accumulate money and return to India and are therefore culturally intransigent.

Irman, who is reportedly worth five hundred million dollars, finds the stereotype of cultural intransigence credible. His technological innovations have revolutionized the world, but he is gaining fame or infamy for issues beyond his technological and entrepreneurial expertise—immigration policy. *Irman* has proposed some radical changes to the family reunification provision of the 1965 Immigration Act like limiting eligibility to spouses and children.[30] He admitted, "I brought my brothers and sisters here, don't get me wrong, but none of them turned out." He argues that the family reunification provision fuels the migration of poor quality immigrants, unlike high quality immigrants like him and many other Asian Indian elites. *Irman* expressed fear over the prospects of family reunification and forecasts that every qualified engineer begets at least ten "poor quality" immigrants who are culturally intransigent and do not achieve the exceptional feats of Asian Indian elites.

Additionally, *Irman* verbalized his discontent with the more recent stream of Asian Indian immigrants to the United States—H-1B visa recipients.[31] He recounted his early days as a graduate student in the

---

[30] Barkan (1992: 69-75) explains that with the October 3, 1965 Immigration and Nationality Act Amendments, three-fourths of immigration quotas were allotted for the relatives of U.S. citizens. Moreover, the first, fourth, and fifth preferences of the act allow U.S citizens to petition for family members. Permanent residents of the U.S. could also apply for family reunification, however did so through the second preference of the act.

[31] The H-1B visa is a non-immigrant visa issued to those in "specialty" occupations. H-1B visas are issued to an overwhelming number of Asian

Midwest who went from eating *chaat* while rooting for his favorite cricket team to eating hotdogs while cheering on the Cleveland Indians. *Irman* attributes his exceptional mobility to being cultural flexible, or put another way, assimilated. Unlike himself, recent immigrants encounter a sizable Asian Indian migration industry that allows them to continue to live as if they were still in India. He noted that they forgo many of America's favorite pastimes, eat only Indian food, watch *Bollywood* films and Indian satellite television, and predominantly socialize with fellow Asian Indian H-1B recipients. As a result *Irman* argues they are at a disadvantage and will not reach the level of success of himself and his generation.

Hence, *Irman's* concerns are two-fold; he not only expresses concern over the mobility prospects for recent Asian Indian immigrants, "poor quality," which even include highly skilled H-1B visa recipients, but also over the impact that their perceived cultural intransigence has on the image of highly successful Asian Indian elites like himself. They seem to give Asian Indian elites a bad name. As a result, *Irman* engages in a very public form of distancing by lobbying for the reform of immigration policy to keep such immigrants out. This establishes just how different Asian Indian elites are from the wider population of Asian Indians in the United States. *Irman,* verbalizing this difference, engages in a curious form distancing or othering from "fellow" coethnics (Simmel 1950; Bourdieu and Passeron1977; Lamont 1992; and Waters 1999). This intraethnic distancing or othering is how the culture of success for Asian Indian elites is constructed. Asian Indian elites are far removed from the wider Asian Indian population and, as *Irman's* comments clearly reveal, are a different quality of immigrants, are a different kind of smart, and possess different social and cultural capital.

While they may seem politically incorrect in our current climate of ethnic pluralism, *Irman's* comments are not "out of left field" or as cricketers would say, "offside." In addition to being stereotyped as culturally intransigent, Asian Indians are also thought to be poor communicators, writers, and speak with an unpopular heavy accents. *Devan,* although a 1.5 generation Asian Indian himself, openly mocked members of the *Indian Professional Skilled Speakers Club* who spoke

---

Indians who are employed in engineering fields. Critics of the H-1B visa program argue that it constitutes reverse discrimination where temporary immigrant professionals are favored over native-born Americans.

with heavy accents or pronounced words in British English. Although he admitted that he also speaks with a slight Asian Indian accent, he still found it amusing to parody it. *Devan* suggests that Asian Indians need to take accent reduction courses so it will make it easier for American people to accept them. He elaborates,

> Having an Indian accent is a problem. Not for me, but for a lot of other people. I think it affects a lot of the things that they do socially and professionally. Thick Indian accents, from what I understand, are not the most exciting thing to hear. Because I know and even I make fun of it. But everyone makes fun of Indian accents. It is like having a thick Southern accents. You know you look at that person differently. Like somebody from India for example doesn't understand the American customs and ways. You immediately know that they are different—the way they look at things and their manners.

Devan's sentiments about the Asian Indian accent illustrate how consequential these stereotypes are; although a 1.5 generation Asian Indian himself, he has internalized the wider stereotype about the Asian Indian accent and associates it with cultural intransigence. According to *Devan,* a heavy Asian Indian accent signals difference in terms of outlook and social manners. Although he speaks with a slight Asian Indian accent, *Devan* argues that this does not cause him problems or affect him socially and professional. He is different from other Asian Indian immigrants who speak with an accent. He is an exceptional Asian Indian elite.

Manraj, known to club members as *Manny,* also associates heavy Asian Indian accents with cultural intransigence. Wearing his signature blue pinstriped suit, this successful engineer turned real estate broker delivered an inspirational speech titled, "The Three, Three, Three Routine." Beyond encouraging the audience to practice positive affirmations and daydream to reach their goals, this speech revealed that *Manraj* is a different kind of Asian Indian, an elite. *Manraj* shared an illustrative anecdote from a recent business trip to Las Vegas. He took a brief break from a conference presentation and decided to try his luck at the quarter slot machines where he came across a "moron" Asian Indian. This type of Asian Indian was the owner of a taxi company, missing a tooth, spoke heavily accented English, and was spitting chewing tobacco into a plastic cup. *Manraj* sized up this Asian Indian and remarked, "You know, he was the kind of Indian that makes you embarrassed to be one." Although *Manraj* also has a slight Asian Indian accent, he exaggerated it and added a moronic facial expression by making his eyes pop out and curling his lower lip to the left when he spoke from the "moron" Asian Indian's perspective.

Manraj observed the "moron" doing "The Three, Three, Three Routine," and concluded that he may not be such a "moron" after all. Yet despite this positive take away message, *Manraj*, like many Asian Indian elites, is embarrassed of Asian Indians with heavy accents, missing teeth, non-professional careers, and an addiction to chewing tobacco. Being an Asian Indian elite is defined in opposition to these unfavorable traits, behaviors, habits. Asian Indian elites like *Manraj* are culturally compliant, smart, and sophisticated while Asian Indians who are culturally intransigent are deemed inane.

Devan and *Manraj* are not incorrect to note that the Asian Indian accent has an affect on the professional and social lives of Asian Indians. This stereotype, along with the others listed above, has consequences that are empirically documented for Asian Indian immigrants and other minority groups in the workplace. According to scholars (Cabezas et al 1989; Fernandez 1998; Woo 2000; Sandhu 2002), this stereotype leads employers to believe that Asian Indians, as well as other Asian minority groups, lack communication and leadership skills necessary for positions in upper management.

Ria, a twenty-nine-year-old software engineer, attests to this. While Asian Indians are stereotyped as smart, such perceptions about their accents can impact their mobility in the workplace. *Ria* details,

> I've heard a lot of stereotypes about Indians. They range from, "Oh, Indians work a lot, that's one thing. People also think that Indians do that more so they get the approval from their managers or create this impression that they are really good. That may or may not be correct. The other thing revolves around the language and accent. People often say to Indians, "I can't understand you or I don't want you to do the presentation. I'd rather have the other person do it." It would never happen on my team—I wouldn't let it. But I know of cases where it has happened.

Despite being analytically and quantitatively competent, the stereotype of having a heavy and unpopular accent has real consequences for Asian Indians. For example, one consequence is that Asian Indians are perceived to lack dimensionality in the workplace and are relegated to technical tasks. *Ria* sees herself as an exception—an Asian Indian without a heavy accent and good communication and leadership skills.

Prashad (2000) documents these stereotypes as well and argues they constitute a form of benevolent racism. Asian Indians are lauded for their hard work, ability to speak English, albeit accented, and docility. Though they are thought to have genetic brilliance, it is specifically for technical labor. Prashad (2000: 71) remarks that like other labor migrants, Asian Indians are wanted as highly skilled workers, but for little else beyond that. Asian Indian elites seem to recognize this and, in response, engage in intra-ethnic distancing or "othering" (Simmel 1950; Bourdieu and Passeron1977; Lamont 1992; Waters 1999).[32] As evident from *Irman, Devan, Manraj, Ana,* and *Ria's* remarks, they define their own success in direct contrast to this stereotype of Asian Indians having technical competence and lacking communication and leadership skills. This is the case with most study participants; they describe how they are exceptional, which is usually in direct contrast to stereotypes about other non-elite Asian Indians.

For example, when listing the stereotype of Asian Indians being smart, *Gary* affirmed that there is truth to it. He contends that Asian Indians are smart, but success really depends on individual characteristics. He provided his own case as an example:

---

[32] Simmel (1950), Bourdieu and Passeron (1977), Lamont (1992) and Waters (1999) explain that identity is relational. This means that it is constructed vis-à-vis another group by making them out to be different. Among Asian Indian elites "othering" curiously occurs within the ethnic group. Asian Indian elites describe how they are exceptional and different from the widespread stereotypes about Asian Indians. This is illustrative of Lamont's (1992) point regarding class separation—moral boundaries are critical in class separation also. While cultural boundaries are reflected in education, intelligence, and the command of high culture, moral boundaries denote character and quality. Asian Indian elites draw socioeconomic, cultural, and moral boundaries against other Asian Indians. They are wealthy, powerful, successful, educated, intelligent, and even of exceptional character and quality.

Once during a meeting, my coworker said, "Hey, where you live do you have elephants and camels? Do you ride them to work instead of cars and buses?" You have to be quick in responding to those types of questions. I didn't get affected. I was smart. When it comes to technical knowledge other Asian people may have the knowledge, but their communication is bad. Their knowledge of English is bad. The biggest advantage that I had was my educational background. It was all in English. I had no problem with the language. Accent, pronunciation, words, getting used to, driving, anything normal, even talking about sports. I was very interested in talking about sports, even when I was back in India. I could relate to baseball, football, and basketball. It all depends on the individual. See, six months after I got my first job in the United States the test writer told me that I was hired because I pointed out a mistake made my firm made on one of their test questions. This question was framed completely wrong and I pointed it out. They were impressed that I caught their mistake. That's why they hired me. That was the clincher.

Gary is different from rank and file Asian Indian professionals. He is smart like they are, but has a solid grasp of unaccented English, strong communication skills, and cultural knowledge of American sports which set him apart. These traits are diametrically different from stereotypes of Asian Indians and they make *Gary* a successful Asian Indian elite.

Another study participant remarked that the stereotype of Asian Indians being smart is true, but similarly highlighted that he is not your average Asian Indian. Although an engineer by trade, *Girish* is rare because he works on the more prestigious side in sales. He explains that compared to other Asian Indian engineers, he is an exception:

I am one of the rare people who chose a sales background. I would say or if I were to put it numerically, less than a few percent are even consider for this option. In actuality the program is one of the most prestigious programs that you can get into in our entire company. It is an elite program and it is the main pipeline from which people move to a c level executive. I presented it as something very glamorous, but it is also very rigorous. Especially in terms of communicating because you have to communicate with customers, clients, and people throughout the company. Ninety-five percent of the time I am talking somewhere or to someone. So if you're just a technical person you are really just behind a desk. I tend to talk a lot so you can't keep someone like me behind a desk. I guess I'm different from most South Asian engineers if you think about that.

Again, *Girish,* like *Gary,* finds credence in the stereotype of Asian Indians being smart. He believes that most Asian Indian engineers have technical competence, but lack communication and leadership skills. He, on the other hand, has personal characteristics that make him different from other Asian Indians. He has what less than one percent of them do—the gift of gab that allows him to thrive in a prestigious career in sales.

Despite this distancing or "othering," *Girish* values the high human capital of the Asian Indian population in the United States. He argues that being Asian Indian brings him great advantages when it comes to professional networking:

I would say that the stereotype about being smart in general as a working professional has some very obvious benefits in terms of networking. There is a huge group of people that you can turn to. In fact there is one person that I met, actually a couple, through Indian organizations or South Asian organizations where they are in the same industry. It is great that they are in a similar industry and we can joke about it. There is also that sense of we can comment about the industry and provide some information about it that would help us do a better job. I am sure that there have been some situations where I've seen some people get jobs or professional contacts that can help them with their business. That this networking opportunity is immediately available to you without any initial work, that it is there for you to pick up upon, would be a mistake not to be take advantage of.

Regardless of *Girish's* opinion about the one-sided competence of Asian Indians, he acknowledges their high level of human capital and how he can benefit from it. Although he describes himself as exception, as few venture into the prestigious and rigorous world of sales, he is able to find the rest of that one percent through Asian Indian professional organizations like *Skilled Speakers International*.

A DIFFERENT KIND OF ASIAN INDIAN: ELITES

The prior section details how Asian Indian elites distance and other themselves from the wider population of Asian Indian migrants in the United States. This section documents how they understand their own success and, again, it is understood as being a different kind of Asian Indian—an atypical elite. To some degree, these Asian Indian elites have a point; making the Forbes list of the wealthiest people in the world, inventing technologies that have revolutionized the world, and serving as advisors to governments across the world do make them exceptional. But such success is typical to this subset of diaspora. Much of this has to due with historical timing. As addressed in the introduction, independent India's culture of science produced a large population of medical professions, scientists, and engineers. At the same time, immigration policies selected highly educated and skilled Asian Indian migrants to fill labor shortages in the United States (Cornelius, Espenshade, and Saleyhan 2001; Varma 2006; Lal 2008). Despite these structural factors enabling their exceptional mobility, more often, Asian Indian elites attribute it to individual characteristics or circumstances beyond their control. For example, when asked to account for their extreme success, they cited their astrological sign, wanderlust, fate, and even god. Ultimately, their scripts of success reveal that they are exceptional individuals and inherently different from other Asian Indians.

Additionally, the coethnic and mainstream media contribute to their self-perceptions of success and notions of inherent difference. For example, their success and mobility being dubbed "the American Dream on Steroids" by the media lends to this perception of inherent difference (Levy 2008). Through an analysis of their success scripts, this research reveals that these atypical elites are really quite typical. And beyond a pattern in the data, this understanding of success really defines their culture of success and is internalized by the wider Indian community.

Suresh's success script captures this perception of inherent success:

> It is not easy to come to the United States and settle down. In fact I have nobody who has followed me, no…. So whenever I go to Kenya I see all my former classmates and all those that are still in Kenya who continue to do their thing. They feel different from me. They say, "I don't know what it is about you." I guess it is fate. There is something about me. Oh, gosh…. When I was filling out those applications under candlelight, I somehow knew what I was doing except I did not know if anyone would accept me. Well, boy I was making a go. I was taking the first step. I said it is unknown territory as wide as it is, but I want to go. It was fate….

Whether it was fated or the result of U.S. immigration policies, *Suresh* entered the United States in the late 1960s after obtaining a student visa. He elaborates that he was money hungry and education hungry so the United States was the perfect place for him. After earning two MBAs, *Suresh* leapt up the ladder of success, starting as an entry-level investment associate and quite quickly becoming the CEO of a global conglomerate. In addition to this occupational feat, *Suresh* is an aspiring spiritual leader. Again, another facet that makes him inherently different from other Asian Indians and, as a result, successful.

While Deepak Chopra is world famous for seven spiritual laws of success, *Suresh* is gaining fame for five of his very own: (1) fate; (2) passion; (3) *DHABIMAN*; (4) stand-up comedy; and (5) collecting historical memorabilia. In contrast to most Asian Indian CEOs, *Suresh* does not share his insights on information technology, war and peace, or latest happenings with his global conglomerate. He, instead, preaches an anti-smoking, drinking, and drug philosophy that he calls *DHABIMAN*.[33] *Suresh* took this message public on an internationally televised religious show. He contends that his public speaking skills and ideas rival those of prominent religious figures in India because he stole the show. *DHABIMAN* was well received and made the headlines of a local newspaper, winning the praise of a famed Indian religious figure.

---

[33] *DHABIMAN* is an acronym for *dharu* and *bidi mana*. This roughly translates to say no to alcohol and cigarettes in English.

For *Suresh,* his success is inherent and because of this he can forgo many established business practices. For example, social networking in the business world often goes hand in hand with alcohol. *Suresh* fundamentally objects to entertaining clients in this manner. When I asked how he manages charming a global clientele dry, he explains:

> If fact I will answer you in this way: if you hold onto your principles and they are right and strong, other people will have to bend and respect them and follow them with you. All these years I have never had alcohol in my home. I have had several business meetings and you won't even find them in this office and I get all kinds of people. And first of all, as soon as I tell them, they respect you even more. So you know they say you are a person of principle and that reflects on the other side of my life. You see even if they make a business deal with you, if you hold onto your principles, I mean it is positive.

Indeed, his principles shape his business practices and result in his success also. He is different from other Asian Indians and even other elites. He seems to have higher morality and spirituality that render him a success in the business world.

At the close of our interview, *Suresh* surprisingly stated, "Before you finish, there are two other things that people associate me with that I want to share with you." He self-reported two additional factors that make him atypical and exceptional: (1) stand-up comedy; and (2) collecting valuable historical memorabilia. *Suresh* is part of the comparison group of Asian Indian elites who are not members of *Skilled Speakers International.* In order to determine whether *Suresh* was a suitable study participant, I had asked whether he held membership in or had heard of *Skilled Speakers International.* While he did not hold membership, he had heard of the organization and received frequent requests to be a guest speaker at club meetings. *Suresh* explained that someone like him did not need *Skilled Speakers International.* While he saw himself as a born leader and had no fear of public speaking, he expressed discontent with the curriculum of *Skilled Speakers International:*

> I really think that every *Skilled Speaker*—your project is about *Skilled Speakers International,* right—is that they really

should experience a short program in stand-up comedy. They must learn that. Okay, I've done it. Forget all the speech making that they do. They really should learn stand-up comedy. It will be more useful for them.

For *Suresh* speech making is not enough; a better route for those intent on improving their communication and leadership skills is his route— stand-up comedy.

The majority of the comparison group echoed *Suresh's* sentiments about *Skilled Speakers International.* Some snickered and others raised their eyebrows at a program designed to give people a skills that many regard as inborn qualities—the ability to communicate and lead. People successful like themselves had no need of such programs. They contend that their communication and leadership skills came naturally or are inborn and this is an area that separates them from less successful Asian Indians.

Ashwin, for example, attributes his success to his outgoing nature. He explains,

I am an Aquarian. Aquarians are outgoing. Well, I also get sixty phone calls a day. I spend about eighty percent of my time talking. I have always been comfortable and I've never had any inhibitions whatsoever. I am a natural in front of large audiences. I think it [*Skilled Speakers International*] is a pretty good organization for people to hone up their speaking skills and abilities. But it's not something I really have a need to do. Yeah, as I said, I don't have any inhibitions or problem with standing in front of a crowd.

Although his comment about being an Aquarian may have been tongue-and-cheek, *Ashwin* distinguishes himself from other Asian Indians. He admitted that he is more successful than they are because of his outgoing nature and inborn communication and leadership skills. While he finds *Skilled Speakers International* a useful organization for Asian Indians and other professionals that need help developing communication and leadership skills, for him it is unnecessary as he naturally possesses these skills.

Most of the comparison sample of eight constructed the culture of success in the same way—difference. Like *Suresh* and *Ashwin*, most study participants, and members of the comparison sample in particular, self-reported what made them exceptional and ultimately successful. For example, as mentioned above, when concluding my interview with *Suresh*, he felt compelled to stop me and mention his hobby—collecting historical memorabilia. He added,

> BBC spent about two or three hours here and made a half hour show about my collection. I thought that it was good recognition. A couple of my pieces... the very first flag that went to the moon and back—Apollo eleven—the moon and back, I have it! Uh...the other unique piece that I have is from Abraham Lincoln's assassination. They removed thirty strands of his hair when they were removing the bullet. I have eleven of those strands, the other ten are with the Roosevelt family and the remainder are with the Smithsonian. Yeah, I have those and I have not come across other Indians with my hobby.

After *Suresh* gave me a glimpse of his collection, he stressed that each item bears meaning to him personally, his business, and often reflects the international migration of his family. He explained that he has not come across a single Asian Indian person with this hobby. He argued that unlike other consumable status symbols like cars and furniture, historical memorabilia does not depreciate in value. *Suresh* remarked that his rare hobby not only builds capital and wealth creation, but allows him to learns about rare things. Ironically this study attempts to document patterns or the similarities among Asian Indian elites, yet the patterns or similarities in their success scripts and observed behaviors is their attempt to be different from other Asian Indians.

Likewise, *Irman* felt compelled to share his very American hobby—learning about the history of the U.S. Civil War. After venting about the bleak straight line assimilation prospects of Asian Indian H-1B visa recipients, he talked about his numerous efforts to Americanize and acculturate after entering the United States in the early 1960s. Beyond watching baseball and eating hotdogs, *Irman* learned about American history and became fascinated with the U.S. Civil War. After many years of reading, his knowledge extends beyond the traditional realm of a Silicon Valley Asian Indian CEO. *Irman* is an authority on the U.S. Civil War and specifically pointed this it out during the interview to illustrate how different he is from other Asian

Indians.   His deliberate selection of an American focused hobby captures his concerted effort to assimilate. He takes pride in his interest in and knowledge of U.S. history.

For some members, four to be exact, public speaking is their hobby and makes them American. They happen to be good at something Asian Indians are thought to do poorly at—communicating and being leaders. While they have no fear of public speaking and are satisfied with their basic presentation skills, membership in *Skilled Speakers International* is their venue to do what they normally cannot do at the workplace—speak their mind to an active audience. *Dr. Batra,* a nephrologists, professor of medicine, and the inventor and patent holder of two lifesaving technologies, explains,

> I enjoy public speaking and like to speak my mind. It is unfortunate that people get uncomfortable, but at some point in your life you just have to speak the truth. You must lay out the way that you feel and at work we have to be politically correct in many ways and cannot speak our minds. You need an outlet for your thoughts and a place where you can just be yourself. If not [*Skilled Speakers*], then where?

It is no surprise that these four members stir great controversy during post-meeting dinners, however, per the *Skilled Speakers International* charter, members are evaluated on their communication and leadership skills irrespective of the topic. *Dr. Batra* and three additional members make good use of this and treat their speaking opportunities at *Skilled Speakers International* meetings like open microphone night. They are able to speak their minds, however politically incorrect, with no consequence during the one hour and twenty-nine minutes of the club meeting.   However, this does not mean that members keep their reactions to themselves; on occasion tempers flared outside of the confines of the club meetings.

The comments of these four members reveal that they not only see themselves as different from other Asian Indians, but also see themselves as different from other members of *Skilled Speakers.* Moreover, they not only other or distance themselves from the wider Asian Indian population, but do so from the wider membership in *Skilled Speakers International.*

Devan, for example, is a fixture in the *Indian Professional Skilled Speakers Club.* Most members regard *Devan* as one of the best speakers in the club and wondered how and why he consistently attended club meetings over the last decade. When asked to explain *Devan* quoted a former member--"I am a speech geek." *Devan* loves what most people and even club members hate—public speaking. He elaborates,

> I've never had that fear of public speaking. I mean someone said that it is up there as one of the most scariest things to do. I don't know what the exact quote is, but many people need to enhance their skills. For me it is like riding a bike. For me speaking is just like picking up a bicycle and riding it. You don't forget. A lot of other people like *Kavi, Saif,* and *Thuy* need help in because they need to improve their speaking and presentations and things. They need that skill to become successful at what they do. I think I've already got that. Whether it's good or bad, for me it is more of an entertainment or social thing.

Unlike the majority of club members who express a legitimate need for communication and leadership skills, *Dr. Batra, Devan,* and two other members do not need *Skilled Speakers.* Despite this, they participate for enjoyment, its social aspects, or even to showcase their talents.

When other members were asked to list members who they thought were good public speakers, the majority listed the very four speakers that expressed no need for developing public speaking skills and were curious about their motives for joining and participating in the club. *Saif,* for example, describes himself as a shy electrical engineer. His employer recommended that he participate in *Skilled Speakers International* to help him effectively communicate in the workplace. *Saif* marveled at *Dr. Batra, Devan, Vik,* and *Nikhil's* extemporaneous and prepared speeches. After he listed these four members who view *Skilled Speakers* as a hobby, he remarked, "I wonder why they even come here. They don't even have a problem with public speaking."

Even within the confine of these two *Skilled Speakers International* clubs, Asian Indian elites define success through difference. They are different from the wider Asian Indian community and even other members of *Skilled Speakers International* because they do not exhibit traits and behaviors like most Indian people. Their hobbies are far from typical Asian Indians who watch Indian films, play cricket, purchase depreciating status symbols, and have a fear of public speaking. Whether to deliberately assimilate or out of personal preference, they seem to select hobbies that typify American culture like collecting American historical memorabilia, intensely learning about the U.S. Civil War, and even public speaking. This study captures the ironic nature of how they construct their culture of success; they understand their success as being atypical Asian Indians. Ironically, Asian Indian elites are typical in the ways that they see themselves as atypical.

A DIFFERENT KIND OF ASSIMILATION: ACTIVE ASSIMILATION

Many of the success scripts referenced above suggest that Asian Indian elites, and the comparison sample in particular, favor straight line assimilation. While generally defined as the process by which immigrants become incorporated in the host society, the path of assimilation for these migrants is largely unidirectional toward Anglo-conformity. As prior mentioned, classical theories of assimilation posit that first generation migrants only acculturate to life in the United States; it is their second generation that engages in the more subtle and unintended process of assimilation (Park and Burgess 1921; Gordon 1964; Shibutani and Kwan 1965; Gans 1973; Glazer and Moynihan 1970). However recent scholarship on assimilation (Portes and Zhou 1993; Neckerman, Carter, and Lee 1999; Portes and Rumbaut 2001; Alba and Nee 2003; Bean, Stevens, and Wierzbicki 2003; Bean and Stevens 2004) present a more multidimensional understanding of the process.

These scholars essentially argue that assimilation occurs in various domains and directions. This is why assimilation often varies between and also within ethnic groups. Although assimilation is still driven by accommodation, largely on economic or material terms, it is not the unidirectional process that it was theorized to be; in the process of becoming American, immigrants change the American mainstream (Alba and Nee 2003; Bean, Stevens, and Wierzbicki 2003; Bean and Stevens 2004). While some express discontent with the idea of assimilation and its implicit message of Anglo-conformity, these scholars affirm its use and call for the revision of theories to fit the economic, social, and political incorporation of many new immigrant groups in a variety of contexts (Bean, Stevens, and Wierzbicki 2004).

This study does precisely this; I extend the concept of assimilation to fit the path of Asian Indian elites who actively assimilate. Bean, Stevens, and Wierzbicki (2003: 95) are correct to point out that with bimodal demand for labor in the United States, current immigration policies seem to select individuals with unfavorable chances for assimilation. However, Asian Indian elites, who migrated to fill one half of this bimodal demand, have favorable chances for assimilating to mainstream U.S. society. This is because most Asian Indian elites had command of the English language upon arrival and a skills set in great demand in the United States. Therefore, they had little difficulty economically and culturally accommodating to life in the United States.[34] These migrants engaged in the much more subtle process of assimilation. As a result, their assimilation has less to do with their economic situation and more to do with a sense of belonging. Yet contrary to Alba and Nee's (2003) assertion, which is consistent with classic assimilation theories, assimilation is not an unintended consequence of practical strategies to improve material and social circumstances in the United States. In the case of Asian Indian elites, assimilation is intended and constitutes active assimilation.

Asian Indian elites engage in active assimilation in the sense that they actively sought out and continue to seek out ways to become American. Membership in *Skilled Speakers International* is a prime example of active assimilation. For example, when I spoke about the nature of my research to a member of the *Indian Communicators Skilled Speakers Club* in the Silicon Valley at a cocktail party, he shared the deliberate strategies that many members undertook to assimilate to life in the United States as professionals. I asked whether immigrants like himself benefited from membership in the club and *Marty*, who recently sold his multi-million dollar hardware processor company, gave me a perplexed look, reflected for a moment, and sympathetically said,

> That's an interesting question, but I don't there are any Indians
> in poverty here. I don't even think that you'll find H-1B visa
> people here. I really don't think that [*Skilled Speakers*] will

---

[34] Alba and Nee (2003) note that compared to low-skilled migrants, highly skilled immigrants assimilate faster economically and culturally.

> help them with what they need. I mean this is more for those
> who want to work on public speaking. For them, something
> like accent improvement classes are a better route. Both Sam
> and Samantha took accent improvement classes when they
> first came to the U.S., but this club is more about fine-tuning
> your public speaking skills.

Marty explains that enrolling in an accent reduction course is one of the first things that Asian Indian elites in his circle did upon arrival in the United States. They were often raised speaking English and even went to English medium schools in India, but wanted to master American pronunciation. He explained that non-native English speakers experience three difficulties with the English language in terms of (1) pronunciation; (2) incorrect use of grammar; and (3) sentence construction. He argued that accent reduction courses definitely help with the first area and explained that it had worked for him. Despite a relatively recent migration to the United States, *Marty's* accent was virtually indistinguishable from native English speakers. The same was true of *Sam* and *Samantha* who had also migrated to the Untied States around the same time.

Although *Marty* seemed confused about my question, his response reveals that assimilation is not an unintended consequence of practical strategies as Alba and Nee (2003) suggest, but is actually deliberate. Asian Indian elites are not just accommodating to life in the United States with language acquisition or by learning basic American norms and values; they are actively assimilating the subtleties of American culture that signal a sense of belonging. Far more curious is the fact that they are assimilating with coethnics of the same social status or, put another way, becoming upper class Americans together.

While immigration scholars often criticize assimilation theories for their lack of specificity and wonder what exactly immigrants are assimilating to, it is clearly evident at *Skilled Speakers International*. As Lamphere (1993) and Alba and Nee (2003) argue, studying assimilation through mediating organizations provides a suitable lens to observe this process.[35] Organizations like *Skilled Speakers*

---

[35] Alba and Nee (2003) forward that immigrant rationality as context bound and contingent. In this study, the rationality of Asian Indian members is context bound and contingent on participation in *Skilled Speakers International*.

International mediate the process of assimilation and provide an explicit context for what migrants are assimilating to. Thus, Asian Indian elites and other members are assimilating to American corporate culture or the "white male leadership model" (Cabezas et al 1989; Woo 2000).[36] Importantly, they elect to assimilate in this way and to this culture. Not unlike accent reduction classes, *Skilled Speakers International* offers the promise of assimilation at a relatively low cost and time commitment. For an annual amount of ninety-six dollar a year and a time commitment of eighty-nine minutes a week, members actively assimilate to the philosophy, values, and behaviors associated with American corporate culture. It is almost as *Skilled Speakers International* offers a neatly packaged and consumable form of assimilation (Gans 1979; Alba 1990; Waters 1990; Halter 2000; Park 2005).

While their process of assimilation is ongoing, many Asian Indian elites reported that assimilating from an immigrant to a mainstream American professional. *Harish*, a thirty-six year-old vice president of a Silicon Valley marketing firm, explains that assimilation takes three to five years for Asian Indian migrants and is facilitated by membership in *Skilled Speakers International*:

> Learning the ropes in the United States takes about three to five years. That's what I think it takes to become established and come to the mainstream. I think this is a transition period, learning the ropes, learning how to work with your American counterparts and you have to make a concerted effort. This is how I approached it: If I have to come to the U.S. of my choice, I think I have to learn everything from how the American culture works to how American businesses operate. So a lot of learning on those points. I think if you want to be

---

However, the small comparison group of eight non-member Asian Indian elites reflects similar patterns. This is probably because as professionals and elites, both members and non-members are context bound by corporate culture. This attests to the generalizability of findings beyond immigrant members of professional organizations.

[36] Studies that document the presence of glass ceilings for Asian Indians, and Asian Americans overall, report that they are perceived to lack effective communication and leadership skills. These skills are key components of mainstream American corporate culture (Cabezas et al 1986; Kunda 1992; Schein 1985; and Woo 2000).

successful here you have to do that homework. It includes things that we talk about in [*Skilled Speakers*]. You have to make an effort to become clearer in your communication. If you carry with you a lot of thick Indian accent—things like that, while small, I think will benefit you if you pay attention to that and it's a lot of hard work. So it was really hard, but I am glad I did that homework and paid attention to those small details. It was painful at that time. Sometimes it seemed tempting to go back to India because I know everything. By the way, I was working there and I was making good money. Everything was going great and I would have had a very successful career in India, but I left all that and restarted here in the U.S. It was my choice, but along with it you have to pay a price to get into mainstream America.

Harish's remarks are contrary to the widespread stereotypes of Asian Indians as economic people who are culturally intransigent. He admits that assimilation is difficult, but a necessary choice if one decides to remain in the United States. Again, instead of being an unintended consequence of practical adaptive strategies, Asian Indian elites like *Harish* actively assimilate.

Vik's assessment of *Kavi* further illustrates the role that *Skilled Speakers International* plays in the active assimilation of Asian Indian elites. *Kavi*, a process engineer turned entrepreneur, is known as the club investment guru. Retired at the age of forty-five due to a windfall of profit, *Kavi* now spends his time traveling, day trading, enjoying his fleet of luxury automobiles. When I asked *Vik* whether there were any benefits to being a member of *Skilled Speakers International,* he shared *Kavi's* success story as a prime example:

He was a very poor communicator, but he was a very determined man. He is an entrepreneur, you know, a very smart man. He is a very savvy businessman, but he always go his way by being very pushy, by being very aggressive, and he didn't know how to temper and balance it. So he a lot of what he has now, which is his tempered mannerism, his very calm, quiet, he is very balanced in his home life and his professional life as a result of what *Skilled Speakers* taught him. And there are many examples of people who have come and gone, actually taken what they need from this club and moved on. And that's all they needed.

Skilled Speakers took *Kavi* to a higher level of success in his professional and private life. Again, this example illustrates that this organization mediates assimilation to the culture of corporate America. Asian Indian elites like *Harish, Vik,* and *Kavi* actively seek this type of assimilation. Once again, assimilation is not the unconscious process that it is theorized to be; instead it is a deliberate or active process.

As detailed in the introduction, actively assimilated Asian Indian elites do not perceive discrimination or exclusion in the workplace. This may be because their identities seem rooted in their professions and they feel very much a part of American corporate culture. In fact many are responsible for the creation of American corporate culture in the companies that they founded or are the chief executive officers of. When I asked *Gary* if he had ever experienced discrimination or exclusion in the workplace, he took issue with the term and question:

> The whole idea of being discriminated against… I don't say— well maybe it happens, but it is not what its made up to be. If I got bogged down to my own ethnic community, speaking my own language, well I could have done that. Instead, I learned to eat fish and meat. It is a person's outlook. Because they have their own dogmatic mindset that the way Americans live is wrong. Then looking at you they say you are from India and have camels and cows—they take it in a bad sense.

Gary's seems to suggest that discrimination or perceived exclusion is the result of not assimilating. His active assimilation from socializing beyond coethics, speaking American English, and eating American food allows him to take what many may perceive as racist remarks rather mildly. His active assimilation seems to give him an American outlook, even when it comes to discrimination. Ultimately other Asian Indians experience discrimination, not actively assimilated Asian Indian elites like *Gary.* He insisted that most of the time, "the monkey is on your back if you think you are discriminated against."

Suresh shares *Gary's* opinion—actively assimilated Asian Indian elites do not experience discrimination. He elaborates, "People who say, well, I am not doing well. Maybe it is because I am Asian Indian. No, not an excuse! Especially in the USA, it is not an excuse." *Suresh* held onto his principles, but actively assimilated by branching out of the coethnic community. Interestingly, *Suresh* disregards discrimination because he has experienced exceptional mobility

As *Gary* noted, having a social circle beyond coethnics is a way that he actively assimilated to life in the United States. *Reena* remarked that the preference of white American spouses for many Asian Indian elites is also a means to actively assimilate. Although chapter four examines spouses and the relationship capital that they constitute, theoretically, interracial marriage is considered the final stage of assimilation. As an Asian Indian woman, *Reena* seemed insulted by choices of many Asian Indian elite men, but attributed it assimilation, upward mobility, and success. She explains,

> See, look at the founder of [*Coolmail*]. Chances are he will marry a non-Indian. Chances are... my guess... because he doesn't hang out with Indian girls that much. I guess Aishwarya Rai would be it. It bugs me that he doesn't feel and wonder what it is about Indian women that he doesn't feel it is good enough for him. He just feels he needs to hang out with non-Indians to make some point.

Perhaps the point that the founder of *Coolmail* is making is that he has actively assimilated. This is inline with classic models of assimilation (Park 1950; Gordon 1964); interracial marriage represents the final stage of structural assimilation.

CONCLUSION: THE ROLE OF DIFFERENCE IN THE CULTURE OF SUCCESS

Ultimately, the Asian Indians, members of *Skilled Speakers International* and even the small comparison sample of non-members, see themselves as different from the wider population of Asian Indians. They do not speak like other Asian Indians, do not eat like other Asian Indians, do not socialize like other Asian Indians, do not experience discrimination like other Asian Indians, and sometimes do not marry other Asian Indians. They instead seek ways to become American. This chapter documents that this process of active assimilation is largely accomplished through mediating organizations like *Skilled Speakers International.* While the small comparison sample of eight non-members, sought out ways to become American on their own terms, others actively assimilated to the culture of corporate America by participating in *Skilled Speakers International.*

Despite elites distancing themselves from the wider population of Asian Indians in the United States, they share a culture of success. Their visibility of holds the wider population of Asian Indians to a strict definition of success. This chapter points out that this culture of success did not emerge out of thin air. And contrary to popular belief, it is not the result of Asian Indians being biologically inclined for success. It is ironically constructed in the acts of distancing from the wider population of Asian Indians and the active assimilation of Asian Indian elites.

The next two chapters focus on the consequences of this culture of success. Chapter four delves into the private world of Asian Indian elites. Beyond their individual and very visible professional feats, their attitudes about gender and spousal preferences also capture how they understand success.

"Singles" and "Withs:" Understanding How Region and Gender Shape Access Social and Cultural Capital

"I know that I have been successful on the job market, but now I am looking to be successful on the marriage market."

--Paul, 31 year-old physician

Paul achieved occupational success at a relatively young age. After skipping two grades in high school, he sprinted through college, and breezed through medical school. He is a thirty-one year old internist at a prominent health maintenance organization. Yet, something is missing in his life—a wife. As *Paul's* quote suggests, marriage is a measure of success and, therefore, a marker of status. And, indeed, *Paul* found success on marriage market with the help of his older sisters and the internet.

There are over three hundred thousand matrimonial websites that help Asian Indians all over the world with this modern form of arranged marriage. This online marriage market helps Asian Indians select a spouse according to religion, internal ethnicity, caste, geographical location, profession, and even astrological profile. *Paul's* older sisters created a profile for him on a popular Asian Indian matrimonial website and he married *Poonam*, a resident at the UCLA Medical School, shortly after. Fellow club members approved of *Paul* and *Poonam's* union as they have commensurate professional status.

One explained, "That's great! He is a doctor and deserves someone good. Two doctors, what a good match."

It comes at no surprise, then, that Asian Indians have the highest rate of marriage among Asian groups in the United States. Data from the 2010 U.S. Census reveals that approximately seventy-five percent of Asian Indians are married with their spouse present. Therefore, beyond their labor market successes, Asian Indians are deemed a success when it comes to marriage too. They take pride in their low separation and divorce rates and are lauded for this by the American polity.[37]

While Chapter Three documents the sources of status for Asian Indian professionals in the workplace and how it is garnered through professional organizations, this chapter takes us inside their private lives and explores how marriage is a measure of success and marker of status within the Asian Indian community and also wider American society. Curiously, how marriage commands success and marks status varies between the two research sites.

In the Silicon Valley's *Indian Communicators Skilled Speakers Club*, marriage clearly enables status building as both husbands and wives collectively develop social and cultural capital. Moreover, by doing this they adapt and assimilate to life as professionals in the United States together. However, in Southern California, wives and women are absent from the *Indian Professional Skilled Speakers Club*. Members contend that marriage, and ultimately the presence of wives and women, inhibits them from building social and cultural capital. Nevertheless, wives emerge in members' personal narratives or success scripts. Drawing on sociological theories of status (Weber 1946; Kurzman et al. 2008), social capital (Loury 1977; Passeron and Bourdieu 1977; Bourdieu 1986; Coleman 1988; Portes 1995; 1998), the public order (Goffman 1971), and marriage (Davis 1941; Merton 1941; Chow 2000; Gerstel and Sarkisian 2006;), demographic data on Asian Indian professionals from the 2000 U.S. Census, participant observation in two research sites, and ethnographic interviews with forty-four participants, this chapter explores why members measure

---

[37] 2.5 percent of the Asian Indian population in the United States is separated or divorced. This is the lowest rate among any group in the United States (Sheth 1995; Varghese 2007).

success on different terms and why they engage in divergent strategies to access social and cultural capital.[38]

DEMOGRAPHIC DIFFERENCES: THE TWO REGIONS COMPARED

Before launching into a lush ethnographic account for the gender differences between research sites, could this simply be an issue of demographics? Are Asian Indian women in the Silicon Valley more educated than their Southern California counterparts? After all, this human capital explanation is provided by many members of the *Indian Professional Skilled Speakers Club* in Southern California—Asian Indian women are usually less educated than Asian Indian men, and therefore fewer are professionals. In turn, they have little need to develop communication and leadership skills necessary for professional advancement. For example, *Dr. Batra* denies that gender is a significant issue regarding club membership:

> I think there are predominantly Indians who are drawn to the club and I don't think there are any gender issues. Um…obviously Indian women have a lot of household duties and have less of a professional need to speak publicly and less interest. It is men that have this need because they are more educated, the breadwinner, or the professional in the family.

Dr. Batra seems to suggest that a gendered division of labor is prevalent among the Asian Indian ethnic group where women's household duties take priority over professional and career development. While there is some credence to the gendered division of household labor among the Asian Indian ethnic group in the United States, over half of Asian Indian women now participate in the labor force.

---

[38] As addressed in chapter two, this study is based on thirty-six ethnographic interviews with members from two *Skilled Speakers Clubs*. Eight interviews were conducted with a comparison group of non-club members. When appropriate their responses about gender in labor market and region are included.

Unlike other immigrant groups in the United States, Asian Indians have historically had a relatively even gender balance (Jensen 1988; Okihiro 1994). Data from the 1980 U.S. Census found that Asian Indian women had a lower rate of labor market participation than women in other Asian ethnic groups (Xenos et al. 1989). Yet those working were primarily concentrated in professional specialties like engineers, architects, mathematicians, computer or natural scientists, physicians, and educators. Data from the 2000 U.S. Census reveals that fifty-four percent of Asian Indian women participate in the labor force. The median earnings of Asian women are fourteen percent higher than all other women and, more specifically, Japanese, Asian Indian, and Chinese women had the highest median incomes out of the panethnic group. These demographic facts contradict *Dr. Batra's* statement, proving that many Asian Indian women are professionals.

However, looking closely at the demographic picture of Asian Indians in California seems to reveal the opposite. Although data from the 2000 Integrated Public Use Microdata Series (IPUMS) captures only one percent of the U.S. population, it is a rich source of demographic data and can be weighted to correspond to the entire population. Weighting the data and conducting crosstabulations of education by gender by the corresponding Metropolitan Statistical Areas (MSAs) initially suggests that demographics may be responsible for the diverging gender dynamics in the research sites.

As illustrated in the table on Higher Education Among Asian Indians by Region and Gender, both Asian Indian men and women in the Silicon Valley educationally trump their Southern California counterparts. However when examining the differences between the educational levels of Asian Indian men and women in both regions, they are proportionally the same. In terms of the percent of men and women holding advanced degrees, the difference by gender is the same in the Silicon Valley and Southern California—approximately twelve percent. Regarding college degrees, the opposite is true—there is a three percent difference between Asian Indian men and women with college degrees in the Silicon Valley and in Southern California approximately one percent more women hold college degrees. Would this not suggest that the trend should be the reverse? If more Asian Indian women have college degrees than Asian Indian men in Southern California, demographically more should be present in the Southern California research site.

Ultimately these results reveal very little about the divergent gender dynamics in these two research sites, except that there is more to this story than demographics. As Sircar (2000:62) explains, "There are dimensions of human interactions that are not quantifiable." Hence, it is necessary to delve into qualitative data in order to make sense of the divergent gender dynamics of these two research sites.

I also note that data from the 2006 American Community Survey indicates that there are more Asian Indian men, foreign and native born, living in the United States than women (Terrazas 2008). However, this demographic change seems to have occurred after I conducted my research.

PARTICIPATION UNITS AND ACCESS TO SOCIAL AND CULTURAL CAPITAL

Participant observation and ethnographic interviews are methodological means to understanding human interactions that are not quantifiable. Goffman's (1971) microstudies of the public order attest to the value of defining interaction practices in ethnographic work. He presents a useful tool to understand individual actions, social settings, and social occasions—participation units. Participation units are the fundamental units of public life and manage co-presence or the sense of being together with people in a shared environment (Goffman 1971; Zhao 2001). Goffman (1971: 14) explains that individuals appear in public as either a "single" or a "with." "Singles" are a party of one, vulnerable to contact, limited in terms of space, and have to externalize a legitimate purpose for their presence (Goffman 1971: 19-21). Therefore, "singles" experience more scrutiny regarding their presentation of self than "withs" do (Goffman 1959). "Withs" are a party of more than one that are perceived to be together, have a personal relationship, offer mutual protection, have more choice in terms of space, but are judged according to their companions (Goffman 1971: 19). Being a "with" saves individuals from the scrutiny that comes with being seen as unaccompanied. Ultimately, participation units reveal the roles that an individual occupies as he or she navigates through daily activities.

Participation units are a useful way to understand how members make sense of their co-presence, or being together, in both *Skilled Speakers International Clubs*. They obviously do so differently, as the gender composition of each club differs. In the Silicon Valley members appear as "withs," and more specifically married couples. In Southern California, married and unmarried male members, appear as "singles." While the research sites are branches of the same professional organization, the ethnicity of its members is the same, and even their professions are largely the same, why is co-presence managed so differently? Are their distinct advantages to appearing as a "with" in the Silicon Valley and a "single" in Southern California? And on the converse, are there distinct disadvantages to appearing as a "single" in the Silicon Valley or a "with" in Southern California?

While Goffman argues that participation units help people manage co-presence, the fact that they vary significantly in terms of gender suggest that they serve a function beyond this. They shape access to social capital and help cultivate cultural capital. Therefore, these questions necessitate a brief discussion of the sociological theories on social capital and cultural capital.

There are many theories on social capital in the social sciences. Whether forwarded as the social relations that increase the ability of an actor to advance his or her interests (Bourdieu 1986), structural holes (Burt 1992), the strength of weak ties (Granovetter 1973), the investment in social relations with expected returns (Lin 2001), bridging and bonding capital (Putnam 1995; Fernandez and Nichols 2002) the product of embeddedness (Portes 1995), or the relations among people that facilitate actions (Loury 1977; Coleman 1990), social capital refers to the value of social relationships and networks. This complex concept is simply captured in the universal idiom, "it is not what you know, but whom you know."

Social networks create links between groups of people through occupational, familial, cultural, or emotional ties (Portes 1995: 8). However, on its own, the concept of social capital does not establish what it actually constitutes, its sources, and who possesses it (Portes 1995, 1998; Lin 2001). Therefore, pairing social capital with participation units makes analytical sense and allows scholars to empirically examine what social capital actually is, the sources of it, and also those who possesses it.

For Asian Indian professionals in the Silicon Valley and Southern California, participation units, or being a "with" or "single," are conduits for social capital. And as scholars (Zhou 1992; Portes 1995, 1998; Zhou and Bankston 1998; Lee 1999; Gerstel and Sarkisian 2006) point out, social capital does not always bring positive results. In the

Silicon Valley familial ties through marriage and children yield positive social capital. This is explains why membership in the *Indian Communicators Club* is a relatively even mix of men and women, many of whom are married couples, and often includes their children. Members gain access to multiple social networks as they make their own ties, create additional ones through their spouses' ties, and even gain fruitful contacts via their children. In Southern California, however, members forward that these same familial ties inhibit the creation of new ones. In the *Indian Professional Skilled Speakers Club* marriage and children are perceived as negative social capital. This makes the club the realm of single men where women are generally perceived to have little to offer in terms of social capital. Therefore, women, wives, and children are noticeably absent from the club and seem to play no part in relaying social capital.

Despite this, the invisible wives of Asian Indian professional in Southern California play a large role in relaying social capital. Social capital refers to the distinctive tastes and lifestyles that serve as status markers and can simultaneously structure inclusion and exclusion (Passeron and Bourdieu 1977; Bourdieu 1986; Lamont 1992). While the *Indian Professional Skilled Speakers Club* is the realm of "singles," even when not present, wives symbolically attest to their husband's success. These themes emerge in the success scripts of Asian Indian professionals and are in line with Bourdieu (1986) and Lamont's (1992; 2000) theories of cultural capital.

Bourdieu (1986) distinguishes between two types of cultural capital: (1) embodied cultural capital and (2) institutionalized cultural capital. Embodied cultural capital is largely symbolic; it includes linguistic competence, command of high culture, displays of cultivated dispositions, education, intelligence, and self-actualization. Institutional cultural capital refers to valued credentials gained through affiliations with organizations. Embodied and institutionalized social capital act as status markers and facilitate entry into the upper-middle class. In both research sites, club members build embodied and institutionalized cultural capital. They are learning to be competent communicators and their membership in *Skilled Speakers International* is a valued credential in the corporate world.[39] In the Silicon Valley

---

[39] As addressed in Chapter Three, *Skilled Speakers International* is experiencing phenomenal growth in corporate sponsored clubs. At several

"withs" of husbands, wives, and children secure embodied and institutional cultural capital together. In Southern California, however, wives constitute embodied cultural capital as they symbolically attest to the success and status of male members. Institutional cultural capital is thought to largely be a need for men.

Along these lines, Lamont (1999; 2000) notes that cultural capital is a major basis of exclusion in the United States. Lamont adds to Bourdieu's theory of cultural capital by creating a set of boundary structures that parallel the stratification system in the United States and France. Lamont defines three symbolic boundaries that elites use to evaluate status and distinguish themselves from others: (1) moral boundaries that distinguish moral character, honesty, and personal integrity; (2) socioeconomic boundaries that serve as a yardstick to measure wealth, power, and professional success; and (3) cultural boundaries that differentiate education, intelligence, manners, tastes, and command of high culture. These three symbolic boundaries bear relevance for Asian Indian professionals in the Silicon Valley and Southern California as they indicate how they evaluate themselves and others. Based on the divergent gender composition of the research sites, these symbolic boundaries are different for "withs" and "singles" and detailed in the following analysis.

SILICON VALLEY "WITHS": POSITIVE SOCIAL AND CULTURAL CAPITAL OF MARRIAGE AND THE FAMILY

Goffman explains, "Some places disallow unaccompanied guests, but welcome the same persons when accompanied; and other places (albeit not many) enforce the reverse" (1971:21). While disallow may be too strong of a description, the *Skilled Speakers International Clubs* in the Silicon Valley and Southern California curiously fit both sides of Goffman's statement regarding participation units—the former is the domain of "withs" and the latter is the realm of "singles." In the Silicon Valley "withs" are made up of husbands and wives and often extend to their children.[40] Here, all club members are married and use

---

Skilled Speakers International conferences, many members have shared that joining *Skilled Speakers* was a requirement of their job. These members typically work in the sales or public relations industry.

[40] Goffman (1971) explains that "withs" are usually made up of two people, but "withs" of three and four people are also possible.

the *Indian Communicators Skilled Speakers Club* to advance their communication and leadership skills for professional and personal benefits.

Unlike the *Indian Professional Skilled Speakers Club* in Southern California, women in the Silicon Valley are not viewed according to tradition Asian Indian gender roles of wives and daughters; instead they are treated as individuals, and moreover, as professionals. This is true even though many women in the *Indian Communicators Skilled Speakers Club* are the wives of male members. Their presence is unquestioned, encouraged, and makes up approximately half of the club's membership.

The majority of Asian Indian women in the club are professionals who work in the Silicon Valley. Their occupations range from homemakers, programmers, engineers, educators, medical professionals, television and radio personalities, high profile executives, to entrepreneurs. Although *Samantha,* the club founder's wife, is a homemaker, she is regarded as a valuable club member and treated no differently from others who are employed. In a casual conversation prior to a meeting, I asked *Sam* and *Samantha* whether they worked together. *Samantha* looked at *Sam,* laughed, and then said, "No, I don't really work." *Sam* corrected her: "But you did help with accounting at one point? Well, she used to help out and she still does in many ways." *Sam's* response captures that he sees *Samantha* as an equal.

For these equal partners, self-development is an endeavor for "withs." Whether enrolled in accent reduction lessons, the Dale Carnegie training program on *How to Win Friends and Influence People,* and even *Skilled Speakers International, Samantha* and *Sam* have progressed through them together. Husband and wife "withs," like *Samantha* and *Sam,* in the Silicon Valley illustrate that marriage fosters positive social and cultural capital. Husbands encourage wives to join *Skilled Speakers* and vice versa, they help each develop corporate cultural capital, and also provide entrée into wider social networks.

For *Harish* is a thirty-six year old vice president of a marketing firm in the Silicon Valley, it is the same way—building communication and leadership skills are endeavors for "withs." Therefore *Harish* and his wife *Manisha* are members of the *Indian Communicators Skilled Speakers Club. Harish's* work involves frequent travel throughout the

United States and wider world, but he always makes it to Thursday night *Indian Communicators Skilled Speakers Club* meetings. While it is difficult to keep track of where *Harish* is, *Manisha,* often informs anxious members of his exciting whereabouts. At the beginning of one meeting, *Manisha* explained, "His flight just came in from London, so he should be on his way to the meeting. He will be here." *Harish* turned up shortly after and club members applauded his dedication. He greeted members and guests and then checked in with *Manisha* about her job interview.

As Goffman points out, "withs" often sustain two different conversations at once. While the conversations between "withs" are available to all members, they do not necessarily join in. And likewise, *Harish* and *Manisha* seemed to catch up with club members while simultaneously bringing each other up to speed on their home lives. *Sam,* the club founder and a Silicon Valley entrepreneurial celebrity, chimed in and asked, "*Manisha,* did you land that software engineering dream job that you wanted?" She explained that she completed her second interview for the position earlier that day. *Sam's* wife, *Samantha,* then asked, "Do you think that *Skilled Speakers* helped you prepare for the interview?" *Manisha* felt that her *Skilled Speakers* training helped during the interview and specifically cited the extemporaneous short speech activities that were done in club meetings. Then she added, "*Harish* and I have been preparing a lot at home."

Harish encouraged *Manisha* to join the *Indian Communicators Skilled Speakers Club* to help her develop communication and leadership skills that would benefit her in the workplace. He thought that *Skilled Speakers* helped him and was just what she needed to express a more confident demeanor. He explains, "I think *Skilled Speakers* is especially important for women. Take *Manisha* for example—each one of us has our motivations in life, I realized. I noticed that she really enjoys listening to speeches etcetera and I would practice with her before I would come and give my speeches. So I suggested that she join also and it has done wonders for her." *Harish* and *Manisha* were happily surprised that this brought them added benefits at home; they learned helpful listening skills and, as a result of *Skilled Speakers,* now communicate more clearly to each other.

Likewise, *Arleen,* a twenty-nine year old software quality assurance manager, encouraged her husband to become a *Skilled Speaker:*

> My husband is um… he is a very different person that I am.
> He is also a little ambitious and he is also doing his MBA. He
> already has a master's degree and we have the same kind of
> qualifications, but I am on a different track. He views in me
> certain qualities that he doesn't have—for example,
> communication skills and networking skills. I have far better
> skills than he does in that regard. And he feels that the fact
> that I am able to be at home, spend time with him, and keep
> him happy, and still keep a job while doing other things like
> *Skilled Speakers* and dancing and stuff. He feels that I am
> able to do other stuff and do a good job. I suggested *Skilled
> Speakers* to him and he is joining next week.

While *Arleen* sees her husband as a success, she points out that she is a far better communicator and leader than him. Although Asian Indians in Southern California largely forward that Asian Indian women do not need communication and leadership skills for the jobs that they do, this is definitely not the case in the Silicon Valley. Here men and women express that these skills are vital, regardless of gender, for success in one's career and family life. Moreover, these skills are developed by "withs" collectively.

Amar describes herself as a skilled professional. She is a microbiologist at a prominent Bay Area biotechnology company. Her husband owns and operates an oil change and automobile tune-up franchise in the Silicon Valley. While she does not see him as a professional, he helps sustain her as a professional through a more egalitarian household division of labor. *Amar* explains,

> I would definitely say that even though he isn't a professional,
> he is a very big help at home. He knows how to cook, so part
> of the cooking is already done when I get home. That's a big
> help. My work day is from 6:30 in the morning to 6:00 at
> night. I am gone almost all day. He leaves at 8:30 and gets
> home by 6:00. So he prepares dinner and if we're home at the
> same time then he helps me side by side.

Amar is an active member of the *Indian Communicators Skilled Speakers Club,* because her husband helps out in the household. This is strikingly different from the division of household labor among members of the *Indian Professional Skilled Speakers* in Southern California. Although *Amar's* husband is not a member of the *Indian Communicators Skilled Speakers Club*, he frequently attends meetings and club events to support her.

These cases are remarkably different from those in Southern California. In Southern California, self-development is an individualistic undertaking. As later detailed, the *Indian Professional Skilled Speakers Club* in Southern California the realm of "singles" where wives, women, and children are largely excluded. Traditional Asian Indian gender norms relegate men and women into separate spheres. In the Silicon Valley, however, egalitarian gender attitudes are the norm and married couples also enjoy greater spousal egalitarianism than their Southern California counterparts.

Beyond illustrating the gender norms and roles that Asian Indian women and men follow and occupy in the Silicon Valley, *Arleen* and *Amar's* comments shed light on a fundamental fact—these professionals are extremely busy (Koch and Miller 2001; Fernandez and Nichols 2002). *Amar's* household division of labor and *Arleen's* attempt to balance her work life, married life, *Skilled Speakers,* and hobbies attest to this. With occupational demands being so great, Asian Indian professionals in the Silicon Valley must maximize their free time. Attending *Indian Communicator Skilled Speakers Club* meetings is a prime opportunity to do this. Once a week for the time short time span of one and a half hours, members learn communication and leadership skills, build social and cultural capital, and also spend time with spouses. *Sam* explains, "One of the things that I enjoy about *Skilled Speakers* is that I can surprise *Samantha* with my speech topics or table topics questions. We usually go out to eat before meetings, but we have so much fun and expend so much energy that we are hungry again by the time the meeting is over."

This illustrates that the *Indian Communicators Skilled Speakers Club* is structurally embedded in the Silicon Valley (Granovetter 1985; Morrill 1994; Portes 1995; Thapan 2006). In the Silicon Valley social and cultural forces are equally important as economic forces. Therefore club member's gender norms and roles, division of household labor, and appearing as "withs" to access social capital, are influenced by the dynamic culture and economy of the Silicon Valley (Saxenian 1994; 2000; Brown and Duguid 2000; Castilla et al. 2000; Cohen and Fields 2000; Pellow and Park 2002).

While one study (Cohen and Fields 2000) documents that the Silicon Valley is a world of strangers, others find the opposite and attribute social networks to its economic success (Saxenian 1994; 2000; Brown and Duguid 2000; Castilla et al. 2000). The technological dynamism of this region requires a flexible system of production that is institutionalized. Silicon Valley firms are open and linked by social and economic networks. This means that there is considerable inter-firm mobility and information exchange. With this division of labor, many professionals come to see themselves as working for Silicon Valley, rather than a specific company (Saxenian 1994). Moreover, they realize the importance of social networking.

On the way to a *Skilled Speakers* event at a large information technology firm, *Vivek,* a young chief executive officer of a up and coming software company, advised *Shaan of* the importance of social networks:

> I do so much of my work from home so I commit myself to at least one networking event per week. This way I make several business contacts that I probably wouldn't working from home. You do a lot of work from home, so you should commit yourself to at one event per week.

Shaan concurred with *Vivek* and listed the professional organizations that he recently joined: The Lions Club, *Skilled Speakers International,* TIE (The Indus Entrepreneur), Business Networking International, and the Business Resource Network. Members understand the importance of connecting with diverse social networks in the Silicon Valley.

That being the case, attending the *Indian Communicators Skilled Speakers Club* as "withs" is not just a way for professionals to maximize their free time, but also maximizes their access to social networks. Putnam distinguishes between bonding and bridging social capital (1995; 2000). Bonding capital forms among people who are usually similar. Bridging capital, on the other hand, forms when people with diverse social backgrounds and interests interact. "Withs" benefit as they have access to both bonding and bridging social capital. For example, even if a spouse bonds with his or her respective gender or members in similar occupations, by virtue of being a "with" both spouses have access to each other's social networks. A number of scholars forward a more pluralistic view of bonding and bridging capital (Reitz 1980; Fugita and O'Brien 1991; Fernandez and Nichols 2002). Like their view, "withs" simultaneously access bonding and bridging capital.

The search for a keynote speaker for the club's annual banquet is an illustrative case of "withs" simultaneously having access to bonding and bridging capital. *Dr. Kapoor, Romala,* and *Sam* were put in charge of finding a keynote speaker for the club's annual banquet that would draw in a sizable crowd. *Dr. Kapoor* and *Romala,* an executive for a well-known internet company, suggested that *Sam* request a fellow entrepreneurial celebrity to take on the task. *Sam's* wife *Samantha* overheard and opined, "We seem to do that every year. Maybe we can get someone different this time. How about someone from *TVINDIA,* like *Rita*? You should ask her to do the keynote speech." Although *Rita* was unavailable as a keynote speaker, this exchange illustrates how "withs" share social capital. *Rita* is part of *Samantha's* social network, yet *Sam* has access to this network by virtue of marriage. Therefore for "withs," even bonding capital can be a bridging network.

In the same way, when "withs" include their children, they simultaneously access bonding and bridging capital. As mentioned earlier, "withs" in the Silicon Valley extend beyond husbands and wives and often include their children. Members of the *Indian Communicators Skilled Speakers Club* in the Silicon Valley understand and embrace the value of communication and leadership skills and impress them on their own children from a very young age.[41] To do this, they crafted a youth leadership program that offers the same curriculum of *Skilled Speakers International* to children who are in elementary, junior high, and high school.

While the majority of participants are the children of club members, the program was open to the public and widely publicized. Members also tapped into their social networks and extended an invitation to many of their friends with school-aged children. A total of nine children participated in the *Junior Indian Communicators Skilled Speakers* club summer program in 2005. On their own, these nine children have bonding capital. They are socially homogeneous as they are the children of Asian Indian professionals and are in elementary, junior high, or high school. With their parents, however, they constitute "withs" of three or four people and have bridging capital. Their parents

---

[41] See Chapter 5: A Tough Act to Follow: The Children of Asian Indian Elites.

have access to valuable social capital by virtue of their networks; many of these children's parents are prominent figures in the Silicon Valley.

Beyond social capital, children play a crucial role in club members' development of communication and leadership skills, or cultural capital. While all of the *Indian Communicators Skilled Speakers* club members speak English fluently, for many it is British English.[42] Their second-generation has command of conversational American English and more importantly, American culture. They impart this knowledge to their parents on conscious and unconscious levels.

Many members practice public speaking exercises with their children and count on them for support. For example, *Saira's* adult children, *Amir* and *Laila,* frequently attend club meetings to support their mother. Whether running a meeting, delivering a speech, or celebrating at annual club banquet, *Saira, Amir* and *Laila* form a "with" of three. *Saira* organized the club's annual banquet in July of 2005. *Amir* and *Laila* mingled with members and guests while enjoying Indian appetizers. As the banquet meeting commenced guests and members took their seats and enjoyed the educational speeches about *Skilled Speakers International* and the *Indian Communicators* club. At the close of the meeting, *Azim* asked the audience to give *Saira* a round of applause for her hard work in organizing such a successful annual banquet meeting. He also invited guests to reflect on the meeting and called on *Amir* to comment specifically on his mother's growth in communication and leadership skills. *Amir* stood up and humorously said,

> Wow, good thing I'm picking up public speaking skills along with my mom. My mom is doing a great job at *Skilled Speakers. Laila* and I notice that she has more confidence and

---

[42] The more noticeable differences in British English and American English are in pronunciation and vocabulary. One member explains, "Some people can't understand me when I say cars. They think I've said cows. The problem for me is that I haven't been coached in American diction. I know British English and I can adopt certain things from American English, but I can't completely start speaking like somebody who is born here. It is not going to happen unless I get trained."

has made a vast improvement since she started last year. We can even tell when she argues with us.

In the *Indian Communicators Skilled Speakers Club* in the Silicon Valley, developing public speaking skills is an endeavor for "withs." *Amir* and *Laila* also benefit by helping their mother develop public speaking skills; these "withs" gain a critical form of cultural capital together—linguistic competence.

"Withs" also learn valuable cultural capital from their children on a more subtle level. *Shaan's* humorous story about his daughters is case and point of this. After fifteen years of working as a high-powered internet marketing professional in a large corporation, *Shaan* started his own company with his wife. He ventured into self-employment hoping that he would be able to spend more time with his family. The flexibility of being his own boss allows *Shaan* to drive his two teenage daughters, *Gia* and *Maya*, to and from school and even to their extracurricular activities. *Shaan* explained,

> Last Wednesday, *Gia* and *Maya* were getting ready to go to a friend's house. I told them that I would drop them off. Since I was working from home that day, I grabbed my blue blazer and put it on over my sweats. *Gia* took one look at me and said, "Dad, we can just walk." I was insistent on driving them, but they were insistent on walking. I got really angry and told them that it was too cold for them to walk and that I was going to drive them. Finally *Maya* shouted back, "Dad, we're embarrassed of your clothes!" I told them that I would just sit in the car, but they were worried that their friends would see me. To make a long story short, I ended up dropping them off and immediately went to buy the latest issue of GQ Magazine. Even though I run my own company, a ten and twelve year old are able to knock me off of my high horse. Imagine that....

Many parents and children can relate to *Shaan's* anecdote about the generational gap between him and his daughters. However *Shaan's* story is also illustrative of how immigrants acquire cultural capital. The second generation plays a crucial role here by providing knowledge about American displays of cultivated dispositions like style and fashion (Sandhu 2003).

Thus, "withs" yield useful social and cultural capital for Asian Indian professionals in the Silicon Valley. Here, spouses and children are crucial for self-development, which ultimately leads to occupational advancement and economic gain. Approximately four hundred miles to the South, however, the situation is very different; spouses and children constitute negative social capital, but positive cultural capital on a symbolic level. The *Indian Professional Skilled Speakers Club* is a site of "singles."

SOUTHERN CALIFORNIA "SINGLES": THE NEGATIVE SOCIAL CAPITAL OF MARRIAGE AND THE FAMILY

As detailed in chapter two, ethnographers do not enter the field with concrete hypotheses to test. Instead our questions, methods, and theories emerge from observation (Glaser and Strauss 1967; Glaser 1992). Accordingly, I entered this research site in *Southland*, California ready to inconspicuously observe and take notes with my blue pen and yellow notebook. Early into fieldwork, everything seemed noteworthy. Therefore, my first visit yielded seven pages of notes, three documents from the field, and eleven business cards. I even made note of my entry into the field—a meeting room in the basement of the *Southland* Public Library. I recall traversing down the zig-zag concrete staircase to the meeting room where I was greeted by *Mohinder*. He said, "Hello there, can I help you find something?" I explained that I was looking for the *Indian Professional Skilled Speakers* meeting. He welcomed me, informed me that he is the club president, and gestured that the meeting room was to the left. I continued over to the meeting room and walked through the open double doors where twenty Asian Indian men and two white men were engrossed in conversation and laughing. Upon my entry the room fell to pin-drop silence as twenty-five heads quickly turned to my direction. As one member asked, "Are you here for *Skilled Speakers?*" I began to answer, but *Mohinder* reentered the meeting room and said, "Yes, she is. This is Sabeen. Please welcome her to the club." Several members stood up and we exchanged introductions.

With more time in the field, I continued to log fieldnotes, which included documenting club attendance. While three women were listed as paid club members on the attendance roster, I was the only one showed up on a regular basis. In fact, upon my second visit to the club, one member remarked, "Wow, she's back for more. I guess we didn't scare her off." I later inquired into the gender dynamics of the club in a casual conversation with a single male member of the *Indian Professional Skilled Speakers* club in Southern California: "Do you notice anything about the gender makeup of the club?" He laughed and then replied, "Yeah, it's predominantly male. I think that's pretty obvious." Although the majority of members are men, half are married. Unlike the Silicon Valley, none of the married members brought their wives to meetings, dinners, or other club related activities. Moreover, they made no mention of their wives. At a post-meeting dinner at a nearby French restaurant, I asked two married members about their wives: "I don't think I've ever met your wives. Do they ever come to the meetings?" Both shrugged it off and then one said that *Skilled Speakers* was just not his wife's thing.

Later, during an ethnographic interview, *Arvind* candidly revealed what these members did not; beyond learning communication and leadership skills, the Indian *Professional Skilled Speakers* club is a welcomed break from home life for many men. *Arvind* explains,

> I almost want to think we just need our separate time. *Skilled Speakers* allows us that opportunity to escape home life for the evening and get away. That's how our post meeting dinners started, to sort of extend the few hours that we can get away and have our freedom. And that's probably why we linger in the parking lot because we just don't want to go home yet. My wife just accepts the fact that I have to go to *Skilled Speakers* on Tuesday nights.

In the *Indian Communicators Skilled Speakers* club in the Silicon Valley men and women or "withs" occupy the same sphere. Together they cultivate communication and leadership skills or build social and cultural capital. However, in Southern California men and women seem to occupy separate spheres. Developing communication and leadership skills is more of an individualistic and self-serving endeavor. Perhaps that is why in the *Indian Professional Skilled Speakers* club all men, married and unmarried, appear as "singles."

Vik, a thrity-eight year old entrepreneur, suggests the same thing. Out of the blue, on the way to a post meeting dinner, *Vik* asked, "Have you met *Kavi's* oldest daughter? She's around your age." I explained that I had not met her and then he added, "*Jasmine* is a member of the

Eclectic Dialectics Skilled Speakers club. She is doing really well there." I asked why she did not pursue membership in the *Indian Professional Skilled Speakers* club and *Vik* explained, "Well, this is *Kavi's* space. I think that having his daughter around could really be inhibiting. Or vice versa. I bet she doesn't want to be known as *Kavi's* daughter. It's good to have individuality and a little anonymity. Well, everyone needs their own space." *Vik's* conversation affirms that developing communication and leadership skills in the *Indian Professional Skilled Speakers* club is an individualistic and self-serving endeavor. Here, co-presence of family members is inhibiting. This is different from the *Indian Communicators Skilled Speakers* club in the Silicon Valley, where "withs," or professionals, their spouses, and children, develop communication and leadership skills together.

While I focused on the positive functions of social capital for "withs" in the Silicon Valley above, here the same participation unit is a source of negative social capital. To a large degree, wives, women in general, and children are deemed a source of negative social capital for male members of the *Indian Professional Skilled Speakers* club. They seem to recognize that marriage has social costs. Despite the income, wealth, and health benefits associated with marriage, several scholars find that it diminishes ties to relatives, neighbors, and friends (Coser 1974; Gerstel and Sarkisian 2006).[43] Perhaps this is why wives, women in general, and children are excluded; leaving the *Indian Professional Skilled Speakers* club a male realm.

Reena, one of the three women members of the *Indian Professional Skilled Speakers* club, frankly states that marriage has social costs for men who are Asian Indian professionals. She argues that these social costs are far greater when Asian Indian men marry Asian Indian women:

---

[43] Gerstel and Sarkisian (2006:17-18) find that marriage diminishes ties to relatives, neighbors, friends, and other people in the community irrespective of class position (similar income, occupation, and employment status). They also state that differences exist between whites, African Americans, and Hispanics, but make no mention of Asians. This study reveals that in both regions, *Skilled Speakers International* members maintain ties to the community as they are involved in the club. However, members of the *Indian Professional Skilled Speakers* Club in Southern California acknowledge that marriage is a "greedy institution."

> I certainly believe that Indian women do have weaknesses. So do many other cultures, but I think and feel that one of the greatest weaknesses Indian women have is our need to possess. You know, to possess somebody comes from our insecurities or the fact that at the same time we aren't that super overconfident woman like white women. I don't think our men can really handle that either. Somehow I am married to one of the most successful Indian multi-millionaires. But then again so many successful Asian Indian men are married to non-Indian women. Maybe it is something in us Indian women that pulls them down and holds them from what they are doing...? So sometimes being supportive means being with him and other times it means getting out of his way. The Indian woman in me wants to pull him down and hold him back from what he is doing, so I always have to correct myself.

Reena seems to suggest that Asian Indian women are culturally flawed. She lists that they are insecure, lack confidence, are possessive, and even inhibit husbands from their activities or aspirations. According to *Reena,* these flaws or weaknesses impel Asian Indian men to marry non-Indian women. *Reena's* marriage works because she knows when to get out of her husband's way. Perhaps the wives of male club members share this sentiment; maybe the *Indian Professional Skilled Speakers* club meetings are a time when wives, or Asian Indian women in general, need to leave Asian Indian men to pursue communication and leadership skills.

Beyond the separation of spheres, the majority of male members and even one female member provide a demographic explanation for why few women join the *Indian Professional Skilled Speakers* club—few Asian Indian women are professionals. Moreover, these members believe that their presence lowers the rigor of the club and can ultimately impacts the status, honor, or approval of men and women within the Asian Indian community (Durkheim 1893; Weber 1946; Portes 1998). *Arvind's* comment illustrates this. He explains,

> The club isn't set up for women. It's more set up for men and professional things. By saying "Indian Professionals" we are already sort of limiting it to men—well, that's how I feel.

> Um, women in our culture are rarely professionals. A lot of
> them are stay-at-home-moms and what not.

Like *Arvind,* most members attribute the skewed gender makeup of the
club to women having lower human capital. Many times over and as
addressed above, members presume that Asian Indian women are
usually less educated than Asian Indian men, and therefore fewer are
professionals. Because of this, they have little need to develop
communication and leadership skills necessary for professional
advancement. This is notably different from the *Indian Communicators
Skilled Speakers* club in the Silicon Valley. In the Silicon Valley,
familial social capital is responsible for creating cultural capital and
human capital. Time and time again, members stressed the wide range
of benefits that communication and leadership skills yield; beyond
professional advancement, these skills make for stronger marriages and
better relationships with children. In Southern California, as mentioned
above, familial social capital does not yield the same benefits.

Gary, a member of the club for eighteen years, discusses this
difference. He is definitely not shy about imparting his experiences
and knowledge of electrical engineering, communication and
leadership skills, club decorum, and his two cents about life in general.
Gary forwards the human capital explanation to account for the gender
dynamics in the club:

> Off and on we get women, but for the most part it is men.
> Indian women…the girls…the different ethnic backgrounds
> from back in India…number one, I don't I think based on the
> types of jobs they do, they don't need *Skilled Speakers* in a big
> way. As many Indian people as there are here, it is still a
> closed community. Suppose you go and you stutter and are
> not able to communicate and someone is there that knows
> your brother or friend—that might make fun of you. Men sort
> of get away with it, but girls are still shy and affected more.
> Some girls have a fear complex. Also their criticism probably
> won't be taken seriously because they are seen as someone's
> daughter or sister.

Gary affirms that throughout the history of the club, the gender
dynamics have been fairly consistent; members are mostly Asian Indian

men. He postulates that unlike Asian Indian men who need to develop communication and leadership skills necessary for their occupations as professionals, Asian Indian women do not share the same occupational need. While examined and proven to be the contrary above, *Gary* is under the impression that there are few Asian Indian women in professional occupations.

In addition to forwarding the human capital explanation for the lack of women in the club, *Gary* made a thought provoking comment about the closed nature of the Asian Indians community. While the Asian Indian population is sizable in Southern California, word travels fast through the overlapping social networks in this ethnic community. Additionally, *Gary* remarks on the double standard applied to Asian Indian women. While Asian Indian men are seen as individuals who contribute valid and constructive in the club, women are not seen as individuals and are not taken seriously.

Another seasoned member, *Devan*, echoes *Gary's* thoughts. He shares his assessment of the few Asian Indian women who have attended the *Indian Professional Skilled Speakers* Club meetings during his decade of membership. Finishing up a fruit salad, *Devan* took a sip of water and explains,

> We don't let women blend in because there's so few of them. And then our *Indianness* comes out. Especially with some of the senior members, which surprises me because I think a lot of them have strong women in their homes, but some of them just can't handle it. Maybe it is also because this isn't something that women want to do—public speaking. Maybe it's a skill that they feel they don't need to learn. But for everyone else in the club, I think everyone feels like those women are their wives or their daughters and then the typical Indian male role comes out. Unfortunately, non-Indian women handle themselves better because they won't put up with this stuff. Indian women, at least the liberated ones, can handle themselves well. But some Indian women get a lot of attention and are here for the wrong reasons.

Like *Gary, Devan* also forwards the human capital explanation for the gender makeup of the club and remarks on the culture of the Asian Indian community. While only a handful of women have attended club meetings in his ten years of membership, he noticed that their presence, particularly when coethnics, undermined the professional climate in the club. *Devan* explains that the *"Indianness"* of male members comes out. He defines *"Indianness"* in terms of traditional gender roles where Asian Indian women are viewed as wives, sometimes wife material, or a daughter depending on their age.

Here, traditional gender roles overshadow the professional status of Asian Indian women.[44] Although numerous studies (Ghadially and Kazi 1979; Dreyer et al. 1981, Gupta, Shah, and Beg 1982; Dasgupta 1986) document that education, and western education in particular, is linked to egalitarian gender attitudes, these highly educated male members largely forward traditional gender attitudes. While many feminist scholars (Sacks 1974; Vogel 1983; Hartmann 1984) have argued that women's labor market participation fosters greater spousal egalitarianism, several empirical studies (Kanter 1977; Hochschild 1989; Ammot and Matthaei 1991; Dinnerstein 1992; Olsen 1992; Behera 2006) prove otherwise—women continue to occupy inferior status in the family and society compared to men.

This is true of the *Indian Professional Skilled Speakers* club. Even when highly educated and professional Asian Indian women attend club meetings, they occupy inferior status to male members. Male members fall back on traditional gender norms and view women as wives, potential wives, or daughters. *Anisha,* the youngest member of the club and one of the few women members provided insight into being on the receiving side of this perception. This twenty-four year old employee of a prominent nonprofit organization dedicated to defending civil rights, explains,

> Yes, the age gap between me and those men is huge. It seems like they have daughters around my age and sometimes they see me the same way. I feel like saying, "I am here to be a *Skilled Speaker.* I don't want a second father!" I mean they do treat me like a *Skilled Speaker*, but I sort of feel there are so many of them and they really act like they are better than the women. Or, you know, you constantly find yourself trying to

---

[44] Sircar (2000:14-15) defines traditional gender roles as the belief in stereotypical male and female roles as biologically based and predetermined. Additionally, traditional gender roles involve status disparities between men and women and separate spheres of activity.

prove yourself to be equal. That, yes, you can handle the leadership here, or you can do this for this position. Or you can give the same kind of quality speech.

Here *Anisha* demonstrates that regardless of her status as a professional, when viewed according to the traditional gender role of a daughter, she occupies inferior status to men within the club. Male members assume that *Anisha* has little to offer them in terms of communication and leadership. Moreover, this suggests that women are thought to have less to offer in terms of social and cultural capital and, in turn, lower the rigor of the club.

While married and unmarried male members do not have to justify or articulate their purpose for attending the *Indian Professional Skilled Speakers* club, women do. As this is the realm of "singles," women must externalize a purpose for attending and are obliged to behave according to traditional gender norms. Even so, their presence and also purpose for attending becomes a topic of discussion among members.

These findings suggest that it is important to look beyond labor market participation and its material benefits to understand the situation of women holistically. Examining the cultural opportunities and constraints that they encounter is a start (Sircar 2000; Behera 2006; Thapan 2006). It may seem illogical that male members who are educated professionals forward "old fashioned" ideas about gender, however understanding their behavior and comments as being structurally embedded in the network of social relations conditioned by the *Indian Professional Skilled Speakers* club provides some insight (Granovetter 1985; Morrill 1994; Portes 1995; Thapan 2006). In the context of the *Indian Professional Skilled Speakers* having a high status profession with wealth and money and having good communication and leadership skill make an Asian Indian professional a good *Skilled Speaker*. These ultimately are sources of honor, high social standing, and esteem within the club. Moreover, these indicators of success in the *Indian Professional Skilled Speakers* club seem to be a man's job.

In the same way, when asked who can fare in the *Indian Professional Skilled Speakers* club, *Nikhil*, a forty-eight year old engineer turned realtor suggested that women are not suited for the task. He elaborates,

Someone who wants to meet people, enjoys people's company, and at the same time wants to be part of the organization and contribute to this thing. Someone who says, you know what, I am going to come and do my speeches. I am going to come and do my evaluations. I am going to volunteer to be an officer when I get a chance. I am going to take part in this whenever I get a chance. I am going to really step up and try to improve my speech, try to lend my two cents to it, my perspectives, my suggestions, my ideas, and typically men do that more. As men, we just jump into it and stop caring about what others will say about us. It must be hard to do, but because I am a man I don't feel negative or bad. It's probably much harder for girls. That's probably it.

Nikhil suggests that it is harder for women to take on the proactive roles that men in the *Indian Professional Skilled Speakers* Club occupy. This seems to be the case, however, much of it the result of resistance from male members. Take club elections, for example; while few in numbers, women are often sorted into "less demanding" and feminized roles like the club secretary and the club newsletter editor.

Anisha describes herself as a strong Asian Indian woman. She participated in every aspect of the *Skilled Speakers* club including serving as a club officer. She enthusiastically campaigned to become the club's president. She explained that several male members questioned her decision to run for club president and even suggested that she choose a more appropriate office like club secretary or newsletter editor instead. When I asked why she thought they did this, *Anisha* despondently explained,

> They just didn't think that I could do it. *Devan* flat out told me I'd lose and then *Karsh* said that I'd be better off running for secretary or newsletter editor. He told me that I wouldn't be able to handle the work. It's amazing how some of these men are fifty years behind in their mentality. If I were a man, they wouldn't think twice about supporting me and I probably would have won.

This illustrates that although *Nikhil* and many male members argue that it is difficult for women by nature to be productive members of the *Indian Professional Skilled Speakers* club, they seem to perpetuate and augment gender stereotypes within the club. By sorting women into "less demanding" and feminized officer roles and overlooking their attempts to be proactive, women continue to be perceived according to traditional Asian Indian gender norms. *Anisha* angrily added that she wanted to recruit "angry, radical, and butch feminists" to shake club members out of their antiquated gender mindset.

When asked to provide a specific example of the challenges gender poses in the club, eight male members and even one female member brought up the same woman—*Raskia*, a forty-three year old divorcée who is an occupational therapist.[45] For three years, *Rasika* was a long-term guest of the club, meaning that she did not hold formal membership. Members revealed that at one point she was an active member and had paid for a membership, but felt self-conscious during public speaking and preferred to learn by observing others. All nine members attributed her shyness to being an Asian Indian woman. Some even cited the role of the Asian Indian community, stating that Asian Indian women are held to different standards. With word traveling fast in this networked community, an Asian Indian woman's presentation of self seems to have consequences beyond the confines of the club.

Devan, however, went a step further an explained that *Rasika* came to the club for the wrong reasons—flirting.

> *Rasika* is no longer in our club. She came and realized that she wasn't getting the attention she wanted and now she's gone. Everybody wanted her to speak, but she didn't want to and made a big deal about being shy. But after giving her so much attention people eventually gave up. After a while people begin to think it is a waste of our time. It gets really old and everyone wondered what she was really here for. So why is she here...? If she wants to flirt she should go somewhere else. I mean this is a great place to network, hang out, and chill, but these types of people don't want to be *Skilled Speakers.*

Devan's disapproval of *Rasika's* flirting illustrates the double standard applied to Asian Indian women in the *Indian Professional Skilled*

---

[45] Although this case illustrates the traditional gender ideology at play, the fact that so many members cited it is also a result of there being so few women members in the club.

Speakers club. While men in club instigate flirting and harassment, *Devan* included, women in the club are held responsible for it.

Even *Reena,* one of the three women members, articulated a similar sentiment. According to *Reena,* flirting and harassment comes with the *Indian Professional Skilled Speakers* club territory.

> I do hear comments and I don't appreciate them. I've heard them to me even though I am not single. You know, they are not appropriate or professional. They shouldn't be made in club while the meeting is going on, but they still get made and people put up with it. It spoils the integrity of the club. It gets very uncomfortable and turns women away. I bet it gets you uncomfortable. I bet that… But if somebody is going to actually judge you on a level where they are trying to court you or whatever, then I don't think that you are out there to speak. I think that people use *Skilled Speakers* to even romance or impress people. Um, it's inappropriate, but I guess it's okay. It's part of it. Why not…? No one has ever complained. I don't think anyone would. I mean they are all adults and if you choose to—well it's like I said—if you choose to socialize too then it comes with the territory. If you socialize with somebody and then they make a comment during the club meeting then it comes with the territory.

Reena's response illustrates that flirting and harassment are accepted activities in the *Indian Professional Skilled Speakers* club. While *Reena* remarks that flirting and harassment during club meetings are inappropriate activities, she suggests that women are responsible for it because they choose to attend club meetings and these are the consequences of socializing. This is clear evidence that women are held to double standards regarding behavior within the club.

Reena's comment is also telling of the relationship among women members in the club. Although they are stereotyped by traditional gender norms, frequently confront derisive comments about their gender, and are even sexually harassed, gender does not seem to be a source of social solidarity for them. For example, *Anisha* and *Rasika* were both on the *Indian Professional Skilled Speakers* club's annual banquet planning committee. When *Rasika* and *Karsh* carpooled and showed up at the meeting together, the *Skilled Speakers* were a buzz speculating about their romance. As soon as *Rasika* left the room, *Anisha* remarked, "I don't know why she came to the meeting. I told her that we didn't need her help at this point. She probably just wants a reason to hang out with *Karsh.*" In response, *Hassan* interjected, "Oh wow, they're dating…? I wonder how he got her to go out with him?" *Anisha,* like the majority of the men in the club, evaluated *Rasika's* behavior as a violation of traditional Indian gender norms. This illustrates that all members, men and women, judge other women according to traditional gender norms. While they may not hold themselves responsible for men flirting with or harassing them, they do hold other women responsible for the very same behaviors.

Anisha, again, expresses this regarding a former member named, *Eloisa:* "*Eloisa* would tell me that *Devan* would drive up outside of her house and just sit in the car and kind of stalk her. She sort of used me as a dumping ground for her grief about him because I'm her mentor in the club." While *Anisha* did find *Devan's* behavior troubling, she seems to come down harder on *Eloisa* for complaining about his behavior. Just as *Reena* held women responsible for the flirting and harassment present in the club, *Anisha* seems to also. This suggests that they too have internalized traditional gender norms, but they are only applicable to other Asian Indian women (Peterson and Runyan 1999; Gold 2004).

Anisha finally assesses that the flirting harassment that occurs in the club makes status differences between men and women quite obvious:

> Women are responsible for putting out the message that they are not here to look for somebody or a partner. They are here for self-improvement, not dating. If they want to find somebody, choose other dating techniques like match.com or whatever. This will make it easier to maintain a relationship with club members. So when women say they are harassed by these guys, it's not really harassment. They just want to date these women and I'm not too sure that their dating techniques are all too fine-tuned. Women end up leaving the club because the guy is going to stay a *Skilled Speaker*. They accept him more than they accept her. So it is much more convenient for her to leave.

Anisha suggests that no matter how male members behave, they will continue to be accepted in the *Indian Professional Skilled Speakers* club. The same is not true for women. Despite their professional status, both men and women assign traditional gender stereotypes to them and judge them accordingly. Therefore becoming an *Indian Professional Skilled Speaker* is a formidable task for Asian Indian women. Whether short-term guests or members, the majority of Asian Indian women end up leaving the *Indian Professional Skilled Speakers* club.

INVISIBLE WIVES EMERGE: THE SUCCESS SCRIPTS OF ASIAN INDIAN PROFESSIONALS

As addressed throughout this chapter, women are largely absent from the *Indian Professional Skilled Speakers* club in Southern California. During participant observation, men made no mention of their wives during club meetings or at post-meeting dinners. Moreover, interviewing them by comment yielded superficial remarks about having gone to lunch with their wives, getting in trouble with their wives for staying out too late, and having plans with their wives that kept them from previous meetings or a post-meeting dinner. As evident from the previous discussion, ethnographic interviews generated much more on the topics of wives and gender equality. The Asian Indian professionals in Southern California framed their discussions of their wives and gender equality in the context of their own success.

This is similar to Kanter's (1977) finding about the wives of corporate managers; invisibility does not discount their presence entirely. Kanter (1977) documents that the wives of corporate managers play a critical role in the success of their husbands by making them look good, providing testimony about their behavior, and even generating business ties through the wives of other corporate husbands. Put another way, wives impart cultural capital and also build social capital for their husbands. In Southern California, the usually invisible wives of Asian Indian professionals serve as symbolic cultural capital and are critical to their definition of success. Perhaps Asian Indian professionals in the Southern California sample are superficial "singles," to gradate Goffman's definition.

As prior discussed, cultural capital is a useful tool to understand how marriage is a measure of success and symbolically marks status. Although much of the literature on marriage and status largely focuses on interracial marriage and status exchange in the context of assimilation (Davis 1941; Merton 1941; McDonald 1981; Chow 2000), it bears relevance for understanding how marriage marks status and is a measure of success for Asian Indian professionals in Southern California.

For example, social exchange theory posits that racial and ethnic minorities in the United States exchange their economic status for a higher social status when marrying white ethnics (Davis 1941; Merton 1941). In a further refinement of the social exchange theory, Chow (2000) adds the concept of racialized relationship capital to explain the appeal that Asian Americans have for marrying whites or coethnics. Chow explains that racialized relationship capital is manifest at individual and group levels and can be an actual or perceived value associated with marrying a particular race. Like Davis (1941) and Merton (1941), Chow (2000: 4) notes that the value associated with marrying a particular race influences one's well-being, self-image, and even desired social status.

Borrowing this logic from these theorists (Davis 1941; Merton 1941; Chow 2000), wives constitute relationship capital for their professional husbands. This means that there is a perceived or actual value associated with being married to an Asian Indian wife with particular characteristics and qualities. Three scripts of success are prevalent among the Southern California sample and capture what is actually valued by the Asian Indian professional men and wider coethnic community: (1) the lone pioneer and the homemaker; (2) rich husband and a trophy wife; and finally (3) the equal team. These scripts illustrate how marriage marks mobility, status, and success for Asian Indian professionals.

The Lone Pioneer and the Homemaker

While touring his warehouse, *Suresh* discussed the ups and downs of the aviation business. Mesmerized by stories that the American Peace Corps shared with him as a young boy in Kenya, *Suresh* made it to Michigan on a student visa in 1969, earned a masters in business administration, and became a global leader in the aviation industry through a chance encounter while working at an investment firm. *Suresh* attributes his success to coincidence and fate. *Suresh* seemed proud of his wife's lack of involvement in his work:

> I don't think I'll ever retire, but I want to help my wife in whatever she likes. Yeah, do what you want to do. She

> wanted to accomplish something to fulfill herself. This is what she is doing in England now…. In fact because she has performed in front of the royal family, too. Yeah, she did it front of Charles and Camilla. She is doing good, okay.

While *Sam* forwards his immigration success story as a lone pioneer in Michigan making a mark in the aviation field, his wife's pursuit of a hobby seems integral to his success. He notes, "After all, she is my wife, so I am not doing any favors. She feels good about me and I feel good about her."

Kavi expresses the same script of the lone pioneer and the homemaker. He leveraged his entrepreneurial profits in the stock market and made millions. This former process engineer retired at the age forty-five. Now in his fifties, he reminisced about the volatility of the stock market and his humble beginning in India and economic and social climbing in Germany, Canada, and the United States. When describing his wife, *Trisha*, he shared that he kept her out of his business dealings. He even kept in her in the dark about losing a large sum of money day trading. He explained, "She doesn't work and hasn't worked. I don't really know what her life is exactly like. I tell her not to worry about what I do and she doesn't. I think she spends it shopping, going to kitty parties, and taking care of our home."

Both *Suresh* and *Kavi's* success scripts detail how they made it big on their own. Their wives played no part in their occupational and economic successes, but reap the benefits of them. Whether a non-traditional hobby or homemaking, their wives' pursuits mark their affluence, success, and status as Asian Indian professionals. This resonates with Fernández-Kelly and García's (1990) study on the paradoxical meaning of women's participation in the labor force for Cuban and Mexican garment workers in Florida and Canada. Many of the wives' husbands in Fernández-Kelly and García's sample encouraged them not to work outside of the home to mark their own mobility or social status.

Rich Husbands and Trophy Wives

Being rich with a trophy wife is another common script of success forwarded by participants in the interview setting. *Vik* is late to the *Indian Professional Skilled Speakers Club* meeting per usual. He confidently opens the door, enters wearing his navy blue suit, glances at his Bvlgari watch, and then apologizes for being late. He has just returned from Bahrain where he made his latest deal with an aerospace company. When asked about his wife's line of work he seemed taken aback: "My wife doesn't have to work. She is a former model and can do whatever she wants."

Six months later during an ethnographic interview and dinner at a local Thai restaurant *Vik* volunteered, "You must have heard about my recent divorce?" I explained that I had not and inquired as to whether *Vik* was okay. He discussed his marital problems in response. He shared that his former model wife was an alcoholic who had been physically abusing him. After a failed stint at the acclaimed Betty Ford Clinic, he suspected that there was more to her alcoholism—bipolar disorder. He then pointed to his perfect smile and shared that his two front teeth were actually porcelain veneers; his wife had knocked out his original set during an argument.

While *Vik's* marital problems are tragic, they are testimony of his affluence and add to his social status. Despite the demise of his marriage, his explanation of it suggests that he leads a Hollywood life and even has an alcoholic ex-wife. Other members who remarked about his divorce discussed how perfect his ex-wife seemed. She was a beautiful former model, and came from an equally rich family. They dismissed their marital troubles as problems of the rich and noted that *Vik* was once again an eligible bachelor.

The Equal Team

The final success script—the equal team—captures the participants' awareness of assimilation. When asked what type of work his wife did, *Gary* explained,

> My wife and I are very different from the members of our club. My wife works with the American public, not like *Neel* and *Kabir* who predominantly look to the Indian community for real estate clients. We understand what it takes to get along with different types of people. Most of our club members stay within this Indian group.

When I asked what *Gary* attributed this difference to, he credited himself: "My wife learned from me. I set the example. I mean I am into sports and have always taken interest in people beyond the Indian community." Indeed, this script of success differs because the husband's success is linked to the wives' participation in the labor force, autonomy, and independence. However, dubbing this scrip the equal team is somewhat of a misnomer as the husband takes credit for the wives' progressiveness.

Fascinatingly, when asked to look five years forward and speculate on where they will be in life, all six of the unmarried participants mentioned marriage and starting a family as top priorities. While ironic in the "single" realm of the *Indian Professional Skilled Speakers* club, this reveals that being married or a "with" is crucial in the their definition of success.

CONCLUSION

While Chapter Three examines the professional world of Asian Indian elites, this chapter provides a rare glimpse into their private lives and explores marriage, gender, social status, and success. This chapter attests to the value of the comparative method in research. Without the inclusion of a second research site in this study, this analysis of gender and Asian Indian professionals would probably have been overlooked. And this is largely the case in the literature on migration; the potential of women migrants is largely ignored (Springer 2006).

Beyond empirically illustrating the role of gender in the success of Asian Indian professionals, this chapter theoretically advances the concept of social capital by pairing it with Goffman's (1971) theory on participation units. Ambiguous aspects of this concept, like what constitutes social capital, its sources, and who possesses it are clarified. In the Silicon Valley, building social capital is the work of "withs," who include husbands, wives, and children. In Southern California, however, "singles" access their own social capital, but curiously build symbolic cultural capital through their wives.

Chapter Five continues with another glimpse into the private lives of Asian Indian professionals and examines how their children's mobility shapes their understanding of their own social status and success.

A Tough Act to Follow: The Children of Asian Indian Elites

It is nice seeing that all of my Indian friends are so successful. Growing up, we all kind of motivated each other. We are all still friends and see each other over Thanksgiving. It is great because now there's doctors, lawyers, engineers...there's anything you can think of. We always joke that we could run a small society together. I think that the support and love that we have from our families as well as other families—Aunties and Uncles—they are like your other parents still. Even the friends I have made in Atlanta are extremely successful. It is very comforting and reassuring. We all kind of know the values and the work ethic and everyone chooses to make their own decision and follow their path. It is very interesting.

--Ana, 26 year old financial analyst

When asked to compare her occupation to those of her Asian Indian friends, *Ana** noted that together they could run a small society. While *Ana* made this statement in jest, it is an apt observation. As detailed in chapters one and two, data from the 2010 U.S. Census document the high rates of educational attainment, labor market performance, and average earnings among Asian Indians. Moreover, in regards to occupational attainment, an overwhelming number of Asian Indians hold prestigious careers as computer scientists and engineers, financial specialists, healthcare professionals, executives, and upper level

---

**Names have been changes to preserve the anonymity of study participants.

managers (Le 2007). This occupational trend can be attributed to the culture of science rampant in independent India. For Asian Indians growing up in India post 1947, career paths were simple—medicine or engineering. Many of these medical professionals and engineers later migrated to the United States through the skills provision of the 1965 Immigration Act.[46]

India's culture of science translated to a culture of success for first generation Asian Indian immigrants in the United States. Chapter three addresses their phenomenal achievements as pioneers in medical, entertainment and information technologies, and defense industries. This chapter shifts focus to the culture of success with respect to their new second generation. While they are not doing poor economically, their parents' mobility and successes are often tough acts to follow.

Most scholarship on the children of Asian immigrants report that upward economic mobility is a central theme in their lives (Gibson 1988; Gans 1992; Kao and Tienda 1995; Portes 1998; Zhou and Bankston 1996, 1998; Portes and Rumbaut 2001; Park 2005). In fact they define their own success and often choose a path for mobility to restore their parent's lost social status (Park 2005:113). This path for mobility is strictly defined by the ethnic community as earning As, obtaining Ivy League educations, choosing safe majors, and becoming medical, legal, or engineering professionals (Kao and Tienda 1995; Zhou and Bankston 1996, 1998; Park 2005; Wang 2007).

While the children of elite Asian Indian immigrants do not face the burden of restoring their parent's lost social status, they continue to be judged by the narrow definition of success rife in the coethnic community. Moreover, they face a unique burden based on their parent's elite status—a level of success that is often unattainable to them. This strict set of expectations from the coethnic community, coupled with the exceptional achievements of their parents, often renders these new second generation immigrants partial failures.

This chapter explores this peculiar form of mobility and its implications for current theories of assimilation (Gans 1992; Portez and Zhou 1993; Rumbaut 1994, 1999; Perlmann and Waldinger 1997;

---

[46] Eighty-three percent of Asian Indian immigrants entered the United States through the skills provision of the 1965 Immigration Act. Between 1966 and 1977, approximately 20,000 scientists with doctorates, 40,000 engineers, and 25,000 doctors entered the United States as professional and technical workers (Leonard-Spark and Saran 1980; Prashad 2000; Varma 2006).

Neckerman. Carter, and Lee 1999). Can existing theories of assimilation account for the curious situation of the children of elite Asian Indian immigrants? In addition, examining how elite Asian Indian immigrants articulate and understand their children's mobility suggests that the culture of success is changing.

UNSETTLED BY THE UNSUCCESSFUL

I spent many hours hearing about, observing, and even experiencing the achievements of my highly successful study participants. Whether part of *Skilled Speakers International* or the comparison group, these Asian Indian elites had much to share about the mechanisms that helped them achieve incredible occupational, financial, and social success. Often, I was not the first to ask them about this subject; their success stories were frequently featured in the ethnic and mainstream media. Therefore, their responses to my questions about mobility were well articulated and are what I call the scripts of success, as discussed in chapter three. However, one line of questioning rendered this usually receptive and forthcoming group speechless, contemplative, and sometimes angry during ethnographic interviews—the achievements of the new second generation.

I asked participants to compare their mobility and degree of success to that of their adult children. For participants with small children, I asked whether they thought that their children would grow up to be as successful as they are. When I asked *Shaan*, he paused for a moment, requested that I repeat the question, and then sternly explained,

> I see what you are after. I work damn hard and—yes—I am above average. I hope that my daughters will become happy and comfortable. I mean, they have everything that they want in life. They feel pressure from me because they know that I want them to excel. That's the level of pressure that they feel. I feel it too. We talk about different careers all the time, but I am not leading them to become doctors of engineers or something like that. I mean I just don't want them to end up working at Jack In The Box. They have to be the best that they can be. Am I making myself clear?

I probed further, "It is interesting that you mention doctors and engineers," but was interrupted with *Shaan* once again affirming that he did not want his daughters to end up working at a fast food restaurant. Although *Shaan's* discomfort and anger over the question is extreme, most participants were uneasy when discussing their children's mobility.

In fact, *Kavi* ignored the question. We met twice and spent a total of four hours capturing his fascinating rags to riches story that took me on his bumpy journey from Karachi to Frankfurt, Montreal, and Los Angeles. *Kavi* was candid about his profits and losses in his engineering firm. He even shared how he went to the hospital to drop off his company's chief technology officer's laptop so he would continue to work while recovering from a heart attack. But when I asked him to compare his occupational mobility to that of his two adult daughters, *Kavi* paused, took a couple sips of his coffee, glanced at his watch, and then suggested that we should get going. He walked me to my car in silence and then said,

> My daughters haven't excelled as I would have liked them to. Isn't it funny how my own children haven't really learned anything from me…? My daughters don't listen to me. They don't want my advice. They take after their mother and clearly aren't as motivated as I was or still am. Maybe that is what happens when you grow up with everything. I have had a much better response with my son-in-law, *Jason*. He happily takes my advice. I pushed him and funded his MBA. Now they live in Las Vegas and thanks to me he is in a more lucrative line of work.

Clearly troubled by the question, *Kavi* politely signaled an end to the interview. Perhaps his daughters' comparably low status career paths tarnish his image and identity as a successful Asian Indian entrepreneur. He attributed their lower occupational mobility to not listening to him, taking after their mother instead of him, and to being overindulged. *Kavi* further shifts the blame by sharing how successful his son-in-law is due to his influence.

This incident perked my curiosity about *Kavi's* daughters, *Maya and Jasmine*. After a *Skilled Speakers* Meeting a member casually commented on how *Kavi* is the go-to-guy for financial advice. I took this as an opportunity to interview by comment and gauge how the

Asian Indian elite community views *Kavi*, *Maya*, and *Jasmine*. I asked if he had met *Kavi's* daughters and he explained,

> Oh yes. I was the emcee at *Maya*—his older daughter's wedding. She married a white guy and *Kavi*, of course, spared no expense. He is having a little trouble with the younger one, though…. *Jasmine* is twenty-nine and still lives with them. If you ask me she is a little too comfortable and really needs to leave the nest. *Kavi* is really disappointed because she is working as an admin or receptionist at one of his friend's companies. He wants me to talk to her and see if I can motivate her to do something more with her life.

Although *Jasmine* is employed, it is not the "right" kind of employment. Being an administrative assistant does not fit the strict definition of success rampant in the elite Asian Indian community. This is evident from the club member's remark about intervening and motivating *Jasmine* to do something more with her life; securing the "right" kind of employment is a measure of successful parenting. Blum (2003: 9-10) documents that in the Jewish American and Asian American communities good looks, high status occupations, and success in the marriage market are regarded as familial achievements that raise parental value on individual and societal levels. Failing on these socially conditioned guidelines are often attributed to parental neglect. Therefore, *Jasmine's* "wrong" kind of employment puts *Kavi's* own success as a parent into question on an individual level and in the wider Asian Indian elite community.

Reena, also found the question on intergenerational mobility offensive, but shed light on the anomic situation of the children of Asian Indian elites:

> Wow, that's an unsettling question. That is my greatest worry—most successful fathers have unsuccessful kids. It is a worry because it is always something that you are trying to live up to. My son is just like his father. He is very into his dad and wants to be wherever he is. He is a ten-year-old boy with a big brain and a little body and he is like his dad. I don't think my daughter is as concerned because she doesn't know the achievements her father has made, the money he makes,

and the success he has. I don't think I even realize it in some ways. Or maybe I don't want to because he is doing well and only a small percent of this country has. He has achieved more than people ever dream.

Reena elaborated on the potential difficulties her children would have trying to following in their father's footsteps. Perhaps footsteps are an understatement; their father, *Rahul,* is forty-three and has made leaps in occupational mobility as an attorney, certified public accountant, venture capitalist, and philanthropist. *Rahul,* also a participant in the study, has entrepreneurial celebrity and is described by friends, colleagues, and the ethnic and mainstream communities as a born topper and born leader. For him, success is a religious pursuit: "The first question God is going to ask us when we die and meet him or her is what did you do with all the time and gifts I gave you? I am just collecting answers to give to God." *Rahul* extends this attitude to his prepared message for youth: "Live as if you were to die tomorrow and learn as if you were to live forever."

This type of success is a great source of pride for study participants. As documented in chapter three, most study participants believe in the ideology of American Dream and often state that they epitomize it. One tenet of the ideology of the American Dream involves each new generation having better opportunities than the previous one (Newman 1999; McNamee and Miller 2004; Moen and Roehling 2005). This lends to the strict definition of success for children in the Asian Indian community; they are expected to exceed the accomplishments of their parents. With achievements and a mantra like *Rahul's,* the bar for what constitutes success is significantly higher for the new second generation. Asian Indian elites are somewhat ambivalent about the success of their children. To what degree are the opportunities that they encounter "better" than those already realized by their parents?

For the children of Asian Indian elites, much more is involved than earning As, obtaining Ivy League educations, choosing safe majors, and becoming medical, legal, or engineering professionals. They are expected to maintain their parents elite status by becoming equally exceptional. Many try to follow in their elite parent's footsteps, others seek entrepreneurial celebrity, and some pursue notoriety by other means. Even so, such feats are largely beyond their reach and set the stage for anomie: pursuit of unattainable goals fosters a state of perpetual dissatisfaction and unhappiness (Durkheim 1951).[47] Hence, to some degree *Reena's* observation rings true—"most successful fathers have unsuccessful kids."

In sum, Asian Indian elites, their children, the Asian Indian community, and even wider society are unsettled by the prospect of downward mobility for the new second generation. This is because downward mobility or status sliding contradicts national consciousness and the ideology of the American Dream; material lives are thought to get better every year and with improve with every generation (Newman 1999; McNamee and Miller 2004; Moen and Roehling 2005). Curiously, for the children of Asian Indian elites, their material lives are largely unaffected by downward occupational mobility; they continue to enjoy and reap the social, cultural, and economic capital of their elite parents. Their experience with downward occupational mobility results in a loss of status. The children of Asian Indian elites may live off of their elite parents, but do so without their own elite status. Before discussing how the children of elites straddle class identities, I explore how they straddle assimilation trajectories.

THE ASSIMILATION CONUNDRUM: A DOWNWARDLY MOBILE MINORITY CULTURE OF MOBILITY

As I detail in the earlier, assimilation is a useful concept when applied appropriately. Here, I use assimilation as a conceptual tool that is bound a particular context – the children of elite Asian Indian youth in Southern California and the Silicon Valley. In review of the concept, assimilation is the process by which migrants become incorporated into the system of stratification in the host country (Zhou 1993). Not unlike the ideology of the American Dream and national consciousness, assimilation often denotes upward mobility, linear progress, learning the ropes, or regression to the mean (Rumbaut 1999; 2011). This is

---

[47] In *Suicide* (1951:248) Durkheim regards insatiability as sign of morbidity and anomic suicide, therefore, results. He elaborates, "To pursue a goal which is by definition unattainable is to condemn oneself to a state of perpetual unhappiness…It may sustain him for a time; but it cannot survive the repeated disappointments of experience indefinitely. What more can the future offer him than the past, since he can never reach a tenable condition nor even approach the glimpsed ideal?"

why it can be perceived as a problematic term. However, when referring to direction of change instead of degree of similarity, it is a useful concept.

In regard to the new second generation there are various assimilation paths that depend on the segment of society entered (Gibson 1988; Portes and Zhou 1993; Rumbaut 1994, 1999; Portes 1998; Neckerman, Carter, and Lee 1999, Waters 1999). The theory of segmented assimilation (Portes and Zhou 1993) posits just that and presents three prevalent paths: (1) straight line assimilation into the white middle class mainstream; (2) downward assimilation into a minority underclass; and (3) selective assimilation where choice aspects of American culture are adopted within the immigrant community.

If we take apart the process of assimilation, it can be understood and analyzed as transfers in economic, social, and cultural capital that create human capital and shape life chances in the stratification system of the host society. By doing this, the nuances of assimilation come to fore. For example, Neckerman, Carter, and Lee (1999) examined social, cultural, and economic capital of the black middle class and found that the theory of segmented assimilation is limited: there is another route to assimilation via minority middle classes. They forward that middle class minority groups in the United States share and use cultural strategies to combat discrimination and distinctive problems associated with middle class status. This minority culture of mobility is overlooked by the theory of segmented assimilation as a possible path for adaptation. They argue that minority cultures of mobility will become increasingly relevant with the racialization of identity, movement into the mainstream economy, and class formation within the ethnic community.

This being the case for Asian Indian elites, I apply minority cultures of mobility to the children of Asian Indian elites and explore the distinctive problems associated with their class. For the children of Asian Indian elites, a key predicament associated with their class is maintaining their parent's elite status and the expectation to be exceptional. As a result three trajectories are prevalent: (1) the typical Indian success story; (2) outsourcing success; and (3) downward mobility into the culture of the *altu-faltu*.[48]

---

[48] *Altu-Faltu* is an Indian term for frivolity, trivial, or meaningless behavior.

The Typical Indian Success Story

Study participants also contemptuously refer to the typical Indian success story as the "Straight Indian Motto" and "Indian Mentality." Here the children of elite Asian Indians try to follow in their parent's footsteps and pursue careers according to the strict definition of success rife in the community. *Vikas*, a twenty-six year old chief technology officer of a failed start-up, voiced his frustration with the "Straight Indian Motto:"

> Let me give you a real life example. I was one of eight people in the nation selected for a prestigious federal cyber service scholarship and turned it down. It was a full ride to the Naval Postgraduate School and my Mom had a fit when I said no because of how selective it was! Do you know that my Mom yelled at me? She said, "Look at how selective and prestigious this is! Do you realize that you are throwing away an opportunity for your future advancement?" Never mind my own happiness and fundamentally whether it is something I really want to even do. That's called the Straight Indian Motto!

According to study participants and the literature on children of Asian Immigrants (Park 2005), the "Straight Indian Motto" and "Indian Mentality" capture the strict definition of success in the community. Moreover, the pursuit of status-laden professions like medicine, law, and engineering is privileged over personal happiness.

Paul, for example, said that a career in medicine was his only option. I asked if his parents were happy when he got into medical school and he explained,

> I think they were very happy. I think that that's what they really wanted. It was a good thing and they were excited about it. I have two sisters. One of them is a doctor and other one was just was just about to go to med school, but switched and went to law school. I think that's something that we all felt. It was just expected of us. We all felt like we had to become doctors like our parents.

Members of the *Indian Professional Skilled Speakers Club* put Paul on a pedestal. He is only thirty years old and already has an established career as an internist in a prominent health maintenance organization. He also comes from a family of three other doctors and a copyright lawyer. To club members he epitomizes the American Dream and their definition of success. Although most club members are highly successful and some hold doctorates in their respective fields, only medical doctors are called doctor. Even at *Paul* behest to refer to him as *Paul* and not *Doctor Paul*, they continued to attach this credential to his name.

Other members shed light on medicine being an apex career in the Asian Indian community. One explained, "Law is a second-choice profession among Indian parents, the first choice being the medical profession. We follow what is called the Jewish model. The Jewish people excel in law and medicine." Another member explained the unyielding prestige of being a medical doctor among Asian Indians: "I entered IIT Delhi, but my parents didn't like that idea. They wanted me to be a doctor because my older sister is a doctor. Being a doctor is very prestigious and they also said that I wouldn't have enough money to eat if I became a physicist." He wanted to be a physicist and was admitted into the renowned India Institute of Technology in New Delhi, but his parents wanted him to study medicine like his sister. Also noteworthy is that despite the dominance of engineers in this study's sample, forty participants interviewed cited medicine as a coveted profession and often provided an explanation for why they did not become doctors.[49]

Thus the power of the strict definition of success and value of the medical profession weighs heavily on Asian Indians and their children whether in India or the United States. *Paul* attests to this:

> Yeah...I think at the nadir...the worst point...when I was quitting surgery residency...I just thought that I am not good enough to do this. It really became an issue like maybe I'm

---

[49] Four study participants interviewed are medical doctors. A number of engineers explained that their first career choice was medicine, however an age requirement in the Indian school system prevented them from applying for medical school. Medical school applicants were required to be at least sixteen and a half years of age, and a number of study participants graduated from high school at the age of fifteen.

not good enough. Maybe everything I've been doing—this ingrained belief that I am a doctor—is wrong. That was devastating. It was definitely the lowest point in my life. I was thinking about whether I should go back or not. But I think the issue was if I wasn't going back, I didn't see any alternative. It was sort of like when your identity is so wrapped up in one thing—which mine was and still is. And you fee really awkward and it leaves you with no way out. I felt like I was dying and that's it. It was ridiculous, but it is logical. It really took a lot of people. My family is awesome. They supported me to get on my feet again. They forced me to apply for stuff and I really thought I would never.… I thought that was it. I thought that my life was a joke. But it works out. It's pretty amazing. I still thought—I am going to be a bum on the street. It is weird that much later in life I have a job. It is good to have a job.

Following in his family's footsteps and living up to the Indian community's strict definition of success was ingrained in him to the degree that he saw no alternative to becoming a medical doctor. Although *Paul* has made peace with his career choice, he admits that his identity still wrapped up in the ingrained definition of success present in his family and the Indian community.

Other study participants from entrepreneurial families express a similar feeling of compulsion as many are expected to take over family businesses. For example, a conversation with I asked casually asked *Vik* how he is doing and happily shared that he is pursuing a masters in business administration. Another member overheard *Vik* and quickly quipped, "But you're rich and already work in your family's company—why do you need an MBA?" *Vik* explained, "Even if I just ended up working full time in the business, I know that getting an MBA will help it grow and is a valuable endeavor. No doubt about it." When I asked him about this exchange during an ethnographic interview he elaborated on his familial duty and having big shoes to fill:

Now my unique position is that I am the elder of my generation and the male elder. So in a way I am sort of expected to behave a certain way as a good example for the next generation. There is a lot of pressure on me as the son of a father that did a lot and achieved a lot, so there are all sorts of things going on. We are one big family and look out for each other. And no matter what it takes, I will do what it takes to bring everyone together and live up to my father's goals. So it is up to me personally, and I don't think that I will drop the ball. But I start wondering when my professors tell me that I would be a wonderful CEO. Do I have the makings to be something else?

For *Vik* being the eldest son circumscribes his career options; he will take over the family business. While he expressed great enthusiasm over expanding their global aviation company and international real estate development company, he also admitted to being jealous of the his younger siblings. "Personally, I am a bit jealous of my siblings. But it is a wonderful type of jealously. It is almost like I wish I were in their shoes and had all those options and less pressure."

Study participants in other "acceptable" professions report a similar drive or expectation to follow in their parent's footsteps. *Ana* is a twenty-six year old financial analyst who commands a six-figure salary. At the close of the market she explained, "For the majority of what I remember, I knew that I wanted to follow in my dad's footsteps. The only difference is that I was an economics major and my dad majored in finance." *Ana* opined that comparing the success of first generation Asian Indians to that of the new second generation is like comparing apples to oranges. The first and second generations experience success in different ways.

> It's hard to make that comparison. I guess it is an issue of how you define success. Um…you know I think we are very fortunate because we are second generation and we didn't have to go through the hardships that our parents had to go through. I think that they are very successful in terms of what they have done and accomplished. I think that they kind of wanted to make something for their family, whereas we want to make our family proud. I don't know if it is as successful—it is hard to achieve all that they have…. Let's just say I don't know if we are as successful, but ours is a different kind of success.

Indeed, the first and second generations experience success differently, but are judged by the same standards in the ethnic community. Ironically, recent migrants who are the children of India's elite class, are able to outsource their success. Realizing that they cannot achieve their parent's level of success in India, they migrate to the United States and are judged on different terms.

Outsourcing Success

The children of elites in India have the option to migrate to the United States and seek success on different terms. This is the case for *Ria* who left India to pursue a graduate degree in engineering in the United States. *Ria* recounted how she nearly failed principles of mechanical engineering as an undergraduate in a Bombay university. Her professor pulled her aside and asked, "How can you fail this course when we are using a textbook authored by your father?" She explained that her father had a lot of prestige in India. After this incident, she tried to straighten out and challenged herself to obtain a U.S. graduate degree. She proudly stated, "I got my masters degree from the top program in mechanical engineering. Here, in the U.S. I am making it on my own terms."

Suresh and his wife were in a similar situation. They recently migrated to the United States from India. Because *Suresh* lived a lavish life in India as the child of a wealthy Indian steel magnate, he finds that life as an IT Project Manager in the United States results in a lower standard of living. Despite this, *Suresh* feels a sense of accomplishment for making it on his own:

> Right now—even in the United States—I am living a lifestyle lower than in India when I was working for my father. I have a long way to go before I live that particular lifestyle or class or social strata that I started from. But I have to say, there is a sense of accomplishment that I could reach a particular level in life on my own terms and without my father helping me. So that sense of accomplishment is there and that's why my parents are proud. I didn't rely on them for resources or anything. I am happy and I wouldn't be able to do this in India.

Arleen's comments affirm this. Her father is the Chief Executive Officer of an Indian computer company. *Arleen* noted that growing up in the shadow of her father's success was challenging. She opted to pursue a graduate degree and job in the United States because they are regarded as prestigious and confer a level of success that she would not be able to attain in India. Like *Ria* and *Suresh, Arleen* is making it on her own in the United States.

While *Ria, Suresh,* and *Arleen* have not achieved the level of their parent's success, they are successful in a new context and on different terms. This is because they have outsourced their success to the United States. In many ways, their situation is similar to the children of elite Asian Indians in the United States; both encounter a strict definition of success, subsequently pursue their parent's elite status, and find that it is often unattainable. The children of Asian Indian elites in India have an option unavailable to their U.S. counterparts—outsourcing success. What path, then, do the children of Asian Indian elites in the U.S. take if they do not follow in their parent's footsteps and cannot outsource their success? They engage in a form of downward mobility into occupations regarded as frivolous, trivial and meaningless.

Downward Mobility into the Culture of the "Altu-Faltu"

Altu-Faltu is an Indian term that means frivolous, trivial, and meaningless. The children of Asian Indian elites that do not follow in their parent's footsteps engage in downward assimilation, but not into a minority underclass. They assimilate into, what one participant calls, the culture of the *altu-faltu*. This is in contrast to the "Straight Indian Motto" and "Indian Mentality" and explains why frivolous, trivial, and meaningless careers outside of medicine, law, and engineering are pursued. After explaining that her children majored in electrical and chemical engineering in college, *Saira* reflected on her children's happiness:

> My daughter is majoring in chemical engineering. She likes chemistry, but it is very stressful. I told my daughter that I will accept any *altu-faltu* major if she does it. But she needs to slow down and needs to enjoy her life. I mean I know that education is the key to success, but the sky is the limit. I just want her to be happy and healthy rather than stressed out.

Saira is cognizant of the anomic state and difficulties that the strict definition of success fosters for the children of Asian Indian elites. However, regarding alternative college majors as *altu-faltu* reveals that veering outside of the strict definition of success is ultimately a sign of failure. *Saira* listed dance, drama, any sort of art, social work, political science, anthropology and history as a few examples of college majors and career paths that she considers *altu-faltu.*

Anisha, a recent college graduate in political science employed in a non-governmental civil rights organization, fits *Saira's* definition of *altu-faltu.* This is no surprise to *Anisha* who explained:

> My dad thinks that I was brainwashed in college and that is how I ended up a political science major. There's sort of a lack of freedom and you have to have a professional job like a doctor, lawyer, or engineer. I don't really know of Indians in the political field. If I wasn't involved in political science and politics, I would have and always have wanted to be an actor. Indian people aren't really in these professions. I guess I am not someone who conforms.

Anisha does not fit the typical Indian success story and, instead, happily embraces the opposite of "Indian Mentality" or the "Straight Indian Motto." When I asked why her dad objected to majoring in political science and a career with a non-governmental civil rights organization, *Anisha* remarked, "This apple has fallen far from the tree. I prefer not to deal with anything military. My dad isn't thrilled about my job. He is really conservative and does not like how [my workplace] sues people and companies." She elaborated that her father's company has contracts with the defense industry and that he opposed her employment in an organization with inimical interests. *Anisha* seems to expect dissonance and embraces it.

In some sense, the culture of the *altu-faltu* is similar to what scholars describe as an oppositional culture (Ogbu 1978; Matute-Bianchi 1986, 1991; Waters 1999) because downward leveling norms are regarded positive among some children of Asian Indian elites. However the application is limited because this is not always the case and the life chances of the children of Asian Indian elites are not significantly affected. They may occupy a lower class than their parents by virtue of their occupations, but are buffered from living a lower class lifestyle by their parent's economic, social, and cultural capital.

Devan, a forty-year old civil servant, is the odd man out in a family of three successful medical doctors. He describes himself as a "late, late, bloomer in the maturing process" who took time to find himself professionally. While many Indians migrate to the United States to pursue graduate degrees, *Devan* did the reverse and went to law school in India. This pursuit is regarded as *altu-faltu*. Prior to the start of an *Indian Professional Skilled Speakers Club* meeting, *Devan* introduced himself to a guest who recently arrived from India. After he shared that he attended law school in India the guest asked in bewilderment, "Why would you do that when people leave India for higher studies?" Devan looked dejected and explained that U.S. employers did not recognize his Indian law degree, but that he is happy with his government job:

> I wasn't sure about practicing law in this country. It was much more than I thought it would be. You have to be really aggressive to work in the law field. I wanted to work in government. Government work is not a big thing for Indians to do. You don't get paid the way you do in the private sector. Um…a lot of Indians are in business and computer science and medicine. There are probably a lot in the medical part, but not the administrative, civil service part. You don't see as many.

Unlike *Anisha* who expects dissonance for not conforming to the values of the Asian Indian community, *Devan* is defensive when people pass judgment on his academic and occupational paths.

Members of the *Indian Professsional Skilled Speaker's Club* often openly remarked on his defensive behavior. One member was deeply offended after *Devan* mimicked and laughed at a recent immigrant's difficulty in pronouncing the word twilight. He vented about *Devan's* behavior: "He needs to learn how to keep that out of the club. I imagine that it is frustrating to be surrounded by people who are more successful than he is in every respect, but come on. He needs to learn how to control his frustrations and be respectful during meetings."

Devan's occupation does not fit the strict definition of success in the Indian community, but he is a member of the elite class by virtue of his parents. This puts the children of Asian Indian elites in a paradoxical situation; they a minority culture of mobility and downwardly mobile when compared to their high achieving parental generation. As Newman (1999) notes, such status sliding involves a loss of prestige, purpose, and affects identity. In this case, status sliding affects how both generations the understand success.

KEEPING A TENACIOUS GRIP ON SUCCESS

The discussion above captures how the children of Asian Indian elites assimilate in the United States; they either follow in their parent's footsteps or engage in downward assimilation into the culture of the *altu-faltu*. Data derived from participant observation reveal that these assimilation paths bear meaning for parental success. Asian Indian elites respond to their children's assimilation prospects in two ways: (1) working with their children to ensure that they become successful; and (2) understanding their children's success on different terms. Because culture is communicated through behavior and scripts (Goffman 1959; Swidler 1986; Lamont 1992, 2000; and Morrill 1995), examining how parents respond the prospects of their children's assimilation is telling of Asian Indian elites and the culture of success. Parental success is measured by how children assimilate.

Ensuring a Successful Future

Only two study participants, *Kavi* and *Ashwin*, seemed accepting of his children's downward mobility. While *Kavi's* case is discussed above, *Ashwin* likewise explained,

> I've accomplished so much. I think [my son] has taken a few traits from his mother that may render him a little bit different from what I am. I always tell him that you know you also need to balance things. Studies are important. Education is very important to all of us, but don't ever forget that the more outgoing you are, the better the impression you are going to give off. I always point this out to him, but at this stage it looks like you can only tell him so much and I am not sure what he will amount to.

Ashwin is critical of his son's personality and seems pessimistic over his future. He holds his wife accountable for his son's demureness and ultimately states that his son's mobility is in his own hands. The remaining Asian Indian elites are not as accepting of downward mobility and work incredibly hard to equip them with tools that foster social, economic, and educational success.

One such tool is *Skilled Speaker's International's Youth Leadership Program.* Here the children of Asian Indian elites who are members of *Skilled Speaker's International* spend two hours per week of their summer vacations acquiring the same communication and leadership skill set as their parents. In the Silicon Valley, for example, nine children between the ages of eight and fifteen organize meetings, learn to think on their feet, prepare speeches, and make evaluations under the guidance of an adult *Skilled Speaker.* In addition to developing these skills, the children attend presentation on communication and leadership issues by successful *Skilled Speakers* from a variety of professions.

When asks to serve as a presenter representing academia, I ran into *Sam*, a member of *Skilled Speakers* whose son was participating in the youth leadership program. I took this opportunity to interview by comment and asked *Sam* which little *Skilled Speaker* is his. He pointed out his son and launched into a discussion about the benefits of the youth leadership program: "The one that looks like he doesn't want to be here is mine. He'd rather be playing baseball, but isn't this a great program for them? Imagine learning all these skills at their age and meeting all these Silicon Valley professionals. I think it will take them far."

Studies (Gottfredson 1981; Moen and Roehling 2005) document that between the ages of nine and thirteen children develop occupational aspirations that match their families' socioeconomic status. Because Asian Indian elites enroll their children in the *Skilled Speaker's* Youth Leadership Program when they are around this age, it may help them adopt the strict definition of success rife in the Asian Indian community. Therefore it is one example of a deliberate strategy that Asian Indian elite parents undertake to ensure that their children aspire to a career commensurate with their socioeconomic status.

Another strategy is enrolling their children in elite schools. By virtue of their class position, children can access a wealth of social and cultural capital from the ethnic and mainstream communities. This is evident in the unique extracurricular activities of the children of Asian Indian elites like patenting.

Although patenting and copyright law are adult occupations, for *Dr. Batra's* ten-year-old daughter, *Sonia,* they are hobbies. Prior to that start of an interview, *Sonia* asked her father, "Can I tell Sabeen about my idea for the patent?" *Dr. Batra* cautioned her against telling me because I could steal their idea. I facetiously remarked, "Wow, *Sonia*—does your dad tell you bedtime stories about the patent process and copyright law?" *Dr. Batra* laughed and explained that *Sonia's* classmate gave her father a brilliant idea that he ended up patenting and as a result became a multi-millionaire. Dr. Batra informed me that Sonia's favorite hobby is working on patenting her brilliant idea.

While *Sonia* pursues this hobby for fun, it is an adult career that she is gaining valuable knowledge about at an early age. Such hobbies prevalent in her youth peer group may translate to a future career aspiration and seem to put these children on the fast track for occupational success. Furthermore, the distinct nature of having a patenting hobby or participating in an activity like the *Skilled Speaker's International* Youth Leadership Program are markers of class and signal elite status at an early age (Bourdieu 1984; Otnes and Pleck 2003).

Success on Different Terms

Another way that Asian Indian elites respond to their children's prospects for assimilation is to understand their success on different terms. The media and cultural place of Asian Indians add credence to the strict definition of success and creates a situation where the first and second generations are judged by the same strict standards. This largely comes from the model minority stereotype: if Asian Indians have made it to the top rungs of the labor market and social classes in U.S. society despite enduring the hardships of migration and discrimination, it is possible for everyone else and, in this case, the new second generation to also do the same (Kibria 2002; Wang 2007). This logic overlooks that Asian Indian elites and their children encounter a unique context; neither generation experience scarcity or face issues of restoring pre-migration status. But because the definition and meaning of parental success is tied to how their children turn out, strict standards still apply.

Moreover, most Asian Indian elites still hope that their children will pursue a career in medicine, law, or engineering, but express greater tolerance of *altu-faltu* careers. Parents rationalize this status slipping by finding positive aspects about downward mobility and reframing them as markers of elite status. This is evident in a conversation I had with *Dr. Pilla* about his children's professions:

> Actually my daughter used to play with my stethoscope growing up but later gave me a really good reason for why she didn't want to be a doctor. She said, "You were never home. You were always at the hospital. This doctor profession is not for me." She gave me such a fantastic answer. Then I said, "Why don't you become a dentist?" She didn't want to. Then she said she would go into pharmacy and I agreed. One good thing in this country is we give our children a lot of freedom. We know that you are rebels and will run away because your friends are like that. I am not the parent that most Indian parents are. I am 180 degrees the opposite.

While addressing why his daughter did not follow in his footsteps, *Dr. Pilla* affirms that the children of elites do not want to and, perhaps more importantly, do not need to make the sacrifices that their parents did.

Reena's comment illustrates this point further. She explains her children do not experience scarcity and therefore are not compelled to pursue high status careers.

> We try very hard, but it is hard to build scarcity in their hearts. They have never experienced scarcity. As much as I tell them that they can't buy something, they know that we can afford it. They know how we live. So I want them to do whatever they want. If they go into charity or art or whatever they think, they should. Letting go is really hard, so I hope that I can do that. I actually feel that they should use themselves the best way that they can. I know that along the way the right career will fall into place for them.

The children of elites do not experience scarcity and therefore are not compelled to pursue high status careers. *Reena* turns *altu-faltu* degrees like art and charity work into markers of status.

Mohinder, a real estate mogul put it more bluntly and said, "I tell my kids to do whatever they want in life, just do something. They have nothing to worry about. All of my hard work is for them. Their career doesn't matter because they are already successful." According to *Mohinder,* his children can well afford non-lucrative professions because they maintain elite status by virtue of his economic, social and cultural capital.

For the children of most Asian Immigrants, being happy is not equated with being successful (Park 2005). A number of study participants expressed this when discussing their limited career options due to the strict definition of success. However when elite parents ponder the prospects for their children's assimilation, they understand success on different terms and are beginning to include happiness. After *Sachin* shared what life is like as an Asian Indian public figure, he discussed his children:

> It's not whether they listen to me and do everything I tell them to. I am lucky that I have five star kids. Their heads are screwed on right. They are really focused and can say what their interests are and you always want to give them room to excel in whatever they want to do. So as long as they are happy in what they are doing, I think they are successful. It is not how they make me feel or how much control I can have over them. That's not the bottom line. The bottom line is, are you happy in what you are doing? Was your day today happy? Do you have a smiling face? Then you are successful.

This reveals that culture of success for Asian Indians may be taking a turn.[50] Once documented as being far removed from the definition of success, happiness is now understood as a central part. Could having happy children become a mark of elite status?

---

[50] Chavez (2005) utilizes case studies to reveal the processual and constructed nature of culture. Culture is subject to change via internal dynamics, history, and societal pressures. One societal pressure, as evident in the case of the culture of success for Asian Indian elites, are children. Corsaro (1997) explains that children negotiate, share, and create culture with adults. In this specific case, the assimilation prospects of Asian Indian children result in a change to the culture of success—happiness is a marker of success and elite status.

CONCLUSION: THE CHILDREN OF ASIAN INDIAN ELITES
AND THE CHANGING CULTURE OF SUCCESS?

This book explores one main question—how do highly successful Asian Indian elites understand their own success? Understanding their successes in the workplace, however, provide an incomplete picture of what being successful means to them. Success is negotiated through their spouses, as discussed in chapter four, and also through their children, which is the focus here.

This chapter captures the forces at play in the culture of success. Parental success is dependent upon having successful children. But because success is so strictly defined in the Indian community and also defined relative to the exceptional feats of the parental generation, it is often beyond the reach of their children. They occupy an anomic state and peculiar position as a downwardly mobile minority culture of mobility. Their assimilation prospects involve an uphill battle as they attempt to follow in their elite parent's footsteps or engage in downward mobility into the culture of the *altu-faltu*. In turn, their elite parents work diligently to keep a tenacious grip on success and also stretch the boundaries of the strict definition of success.

CHAPTER SIX
Conclusion

I began this book with a discussion about the myths and realities that surround international migration. Overall, international migrants account for a small percent of the world's population, but this small percent makes a profound impact on the world (Rumbaut 2008; Cornell and Hartmann 2007; Bean and Lee 2010). This is clearly evident in the sample at the heart of this book – Asian Indian elites. A few scholars have studied Asian Indian elites (Fernandez 1998; Saxenian 1999, 2001; Bagchi 2001; Cornelius, Espenshade, and Salehyan 2001; Varma 2006), however this research is different. As elaborated in chapter two, the inductive nature of ethnography lends to novelty. Therefore this research departs from common questions about immigrants and labor market competition to a more nuanced look at the culture of success among Asian Indian elites in Southern California and the Silicon Valley.

As prior mentioned, the population of Asian Indians in the United States continues to grow and is increasingly visible. In the last ten years Asian Indians have grown from being a little over half a percent of the U.S. population to close to one percent. Additionally, two current U.S. state governors, Bobby Jindal of Louisiana and Nikki Haley of South Carolina, are Asian Indian.[51] The situation in 2012 for Asian Indians seems far different from the days when Bhagat Singh Thind negotiated the rights to citizenship for Asian Indians.[52] Today it

---

[51] Following the patterns documented in this study, both Jindal and Haley have Anglicized their first names and identify with republican political ideologies.

[52] In 1923 Bhagat Singh f argued that as an Indian he was part of the Caucasian race and therefore eligible for U.S. citizenship. However the U.S. Supreme Court ruled that Asian Indians were not Caucasian in "common understanding" and therefore ineligible for citizenship.

can be beneficial to be Indian. For example, when I asked a San Francisco Bay Area venture capitalist what he looks for in job candidates, he said, "Every successful start up in the Valley needs to have an Indian in a high position." This designation of success, provides a warrant for its study. In fact more research should focus on culture, identity, and assimilation in addition to themes of economic mobility and inter-group competition.

This book is also innovative in the sense that each chapter of offers implications for research methods, extends theories and sharpens concepts, and provides insights to workplace and immigration policies.

Chapter two accomplishes two tasks: (1) it details the objective research methods of this dissertation; and (2) offers a "confessional tale" involving the more subjective aspects of managing my role as a researcher. As explained in chapter two, ethnography allows for the systematic observation of social situations and subjects in their natural environments. Ethnographers are able to understand the meaning of social phenomena, actions, and behaviors to subjects (Weick 1985; Blumer 1969; Katz 1997; Morrill and Fine 1997). Allowing data from complete participant observation to drive all aspects of this study made it fruitful; the culture of success for Asian Indian elites is documented and understood as they themselves understand it. This chapter also addresses the problems and pitfalls that ethnographers often encounter in the field. Other scholars may look to this chapter for methodological insights on studying up, the reality of being an ethnic insider, and how to manage gender relations in the field.

This method fueled the subsequent empirical chapters that examine how success is not only negotiated in the public or professional arena, but in the private social worlds of elites. Chapter three examines the success scripts of Asian Indian elites. While the challenge of most studies that focus on elites is disentangling them from their prepared scripts, this study instead examines them in terms of their meaning and function. Asian Indian elites engage in distancing or "othering" from the wider population of Asian Indians. They see themselves and their success as atypical and engage in a curious form of assimilation where they actively seek out ways to Americanize. Membership in *Skilled Speakers International* is one of the ways that members actively assimilate. Ironically, the wider population of Asian Indians in the United States adheres to this culture of success that is constructed through in the act of distancing and "othering" from them. This chapter addresses a weakness in assimilation as a theory and concept by specifying how and what Asian Indian elites are assimilating to. It also suggests that contrary to classic theories of assimilation, first generation migrants do not simply accommodate to life in the United States, but actively assimilation. Assimilation is theorized to be the modal path of the children of immigrants, not the first generation.

Chapter four borrows the theoretical concepts of participation units from symbolic interactionism and applies them to two related concepts from economic sociology: social and cultural capital. Using these concepts to understand why gender dynamics differ between the two research sites reveals that spouses constitute and generate capital whether present or not. Due to the differences between the labor market of the Silicon Valley and Southern California, spouses can foster or inhibit access to social and cultural capital. Moreover, Asian Indian elites define their success beyond their professional feats; spouses and the mobility of their new second generation are also major determinants of it.

Chapter five, like chapter three, offers a new path of assimilation for the children of Asian Indian elites. Like Neckerman, Carter, and Lee (1999) who problematize the tripartite model of segmented assimilation and forward a fourth path for minority cultures of mobility, this chapter presents the assimilation conundrum of the new second generation of Asian Indian elites: while they are not doing poorly economically, the mobility and exceptional success of their parents are often tough acts to follow. As a result, they engage in a peculiar form assimilation as a downwardly mobile minority culture of mobility. Despite this, Asian Indian elites keep a tenacious grip on success by reframing what the culture of success means. While chapter three documents that the culture of success for them defines success in a strict manner, happiness is at the heart of their definition of success for their children. This stretches the boundaries of how success in defined.

Thus the chapters do justice to the research questions at the heart of this book: (1) how do highly successful Asian Indian elites understand their own success; and (2) how does culture benefit and constrain their everyday lives? After three years of participant observation, thirty-six in-depth interviews with members of *Skilled Speakers International* and eight with a comparison sample of non-members, and a number of years analyzing data, the answers are manifest in this six chapter book. In a nutshell, Asian Indian elites construct their culture of success vis-à-vis the wider population of

Asian Indians in the United States. Beyond their very public professional successes, their spousal selection and the mobility of their new second generation are critical dimensions of how they understand their own success.

POLICY IMPLICATIONS

As discussed in chapter three, the most common way that immigrants gain authorized entry and eventual permanent residence in the United States is through the family reunification provisions of current immigration policies. This occurs despite the original intent of U.S. immigration Acts—to acquire skilled labor (Xenos, Barringer, and Levin 1989; Barkan 1992).[53] In comparison to visas allotted for family reunification, far less are issued to high skilled migrants who enter the United States through the skills provision of 1952 and 1990 Immigration Acts. As a result some policymakers suggest that the United States adopt a points based immigration system, like in Australia, Canada, and Great Britain, that would select a greater number of highly skilled immigrants who generally experience a more favorable incorporation in the United States. As referenced in chapter three, one study participant, *Irman*, is in favor of this policy change.

Irman proposes that family reunification be limited to spouses and children.[54] He admitted, "I brought my brothers and sisters here, don't get me wrong, but none of them turned out." He argues that the family reunification provision fuels the migration of poor quality immigrants, unlike high quality immigrants like him and many other Asian Indian elites. *Irman* expressed fear over the prospects of family reunification and forecasts that every qualified engineer begets at least ten "poor quality" immigrants who are culturally intransigent and do not achieve the exceptional feats of Asian Indian elites.

---

[53] Data from the Department of Homeland Security reveals that approximately 480,000 visas are issued on the basis of family reunification verses 140,000 for high skilled migrants.

[54] Barkan (1992: 69-75) explains that with the October 3, 1965 Immigration and Nationality Act Amendments, three-fourths of immigration quotas were allotted for the relatives of U.S. citizens. Moreover, the first, fourth, and fifth preferences of the act allow U.S citizens to petition for family members. Permanent residents of the U.S. could also apply for family reunification, however did so through the second preference of the act.

Although no one other than *Irman* proposed changes specific to the family reunification provision of U.S. immigration policy, many hoped that the U.S. would follow Australia, Canada, and Great Britain and adopt a points based system. *Amitabh*, described the ease of migrating to countries like Australia, Canada, Great Britain, and Israel because of their points systems. He elaborates,

> I think that the whole system is not really working and should be changed. I think ideally it should be something like countries like Canada, Australia, or the United Kingdom. They have a general qualification like if you have certain things like in Canada a points system. Let's say you have a Ph.D. like myself then you get a number of points. If you work in a certain industry, then you get some points. They add them all up to a certain threshold and then you get permanent residence there. It seems like the U.S. has a broken system that causes problems for Indians and Chinese, but I guess that is not intentional.

Although *Amitabh* expresses discontent over the annual quotas for H-1B visas, difficulty over converting temporary visas into permanent residence, and general uncertainty rife in the program, he sees these issues as systemic problems and nothing personal. Nevertheless, this research, as evident in these comments, illustrates the need for policymakers to examine the human impact these systemic flaws can have. Sahoo et al (2010: 306) point out that immigration policies like the H-1B visa program in the United States pay little attention to issues of wage inequity, the psychological impacts of being in a situation where migrants are 'neither here nor there,' and the wider impact on countries of origin.

Former president, George W. Bush, recognized the need for federal immigration reform in the United States. In his January 7th, 2004 presidential address to the nation he stated that, "The United States needs an immigration system that serves the American economy and reflects the American Dream." The unrealized reforms focused on a guestworker program for low skilled unauthorized migrants. Again, with the exception of strengthening the U.S. borders post September 11th, which makes migration for international students and high skilled workers more challenging, these reforms widely overlooked the issue of high skilled migrants.

Similarly, the current administration carefully negotiates migration as a social problem and social solution. While states like Arizona and Alabama have enacted restrictionary immigration policies to preserve jobs for Americans, President Obama has called for Congress to increase the number of green cards for high skilled immigrant workers. Despite the current downturn in the economy, the Obama administration is looking to high skilled immigration as a social solution. To spur job growth the president supports "An Entrepreneurs in Residence" program which will create a special visa category for immigrants who intend to create start-ups (Thibodeau 2011). Hence, the current administration must carefully craft immigration policies that make the United States competitive, while keeping the general public's fears of displacement at bay (Paxton et al 2006).

Beyond extending sociological theory, this book illustrates the benefit of retaining the population of immigrants in the United States and on student and H-1B visas. Many corporations like Apple, Microsoft, Google, Motorola, Intel, Oracle, and Hewlett-Packard rely on high skilled immigrants to remain competitive. In 2007 Bill Gates testified before Congress and urged for more flexibility immigration policies regarding the highly skilled. Gates issued the following decree: "Simply put: it makes no sense to tell well-trained, highly skilled individuals—many of whom are educated at our top colleges and universities that the United States does not welcome or value them" (*Businessweek* 2007).

While the general public and conservative policymakers express concern over immigrant and native competition for jobs, the overall contributions of high skilled immigrants make this nation more prosperity and actually lead to jobs creation. Despite this, the debate will become increasingly contentious in light of the recent economic downturn and resulting high unemployment. With the increased scrutiny over applicants for student visas, the United States may need to alter immigration policies to access and retain high skilled workers in the highly competitive global labor market (Kasarda 1995; Wilson 1987).

This research also has policy implications for workplace diversity and inclusion initiatives. Motivated by globalization, approximately three-quarters of all large corporations have diversity programs. They argue that the high costs associated with such programs are necessary and result in increased profits; companies committed to diversity report better relations in the business world and argue that it allows them to attract and retain strong talent (Pernula 2008). *Skilled Speakers International* is growing part of corporate diversity programs, in the sense that it assimilates workers, both foreign and native born, to corporate culture.

As noted in chapter two, *Skilled Speakers* is experiencing phenomenal growth in corporations. More than one thousand major corporations sponsor "in house" clubs that offer training and workshops to their employees. These corporations range from information technology companies, like Intel and Microsoft, to agencies within the U.S. government like the Department of Justice and the Food and Drug Administration, and even universities. While the majority of study participants joined *Skilled Speakers* on their own volition, or to actively assimilation, for many sales and public relations professionals membership is a job requirement. In these industries employers will cover membership dues and often pay their employees to attend.

While this study focuses on how *Skilled Speakers* is a site for assimilation to life in the United States and the culture of corporate America, the interaction of migrants and native born workers in this context is noteworthy. While immigration scholars (Lamphere 1993) argue that low skilled migrants and native born Americans live in divided social worlds, the case is very different for the highly skilled and their American counterparts. To what degree, then, does *Skilled Speakers International* in corporations assimilate immigrants and also serve as diversity training? However in order to empirically assess this, future research that focuses on corporate sponsored *Skilled Speakers* clubs is necessary.

On a related note, in the Silicon Valley some companies closely guard data on the diversity of their workforces. While they forward EEOC compliant statements about valuing diversity on their websites, they refuse to release the actual demographics of their respective companies, citing the diversity or their workforce as a trade secret (Swift 2010; Pepitone 2011). Researching *Skilled Speakers International* corporate clubs and Asian Indian employees at these particular companies may be analytically useful.

DIRECTIONS FOR FUTURE RESEARCH

Despite the length of time that I spent in the field, an impressive data yield, and this book, I still have more questions than answers, which are suitable directions for future research. As addressed above, this book is a critical case study with two research sites. Expanding beyond these specialized clubs for Asian Indians may yield a fruitful and comparative dimension. Perhaps corporate sponsored clubs or clubs catering to a different ethnic group in the United States may yield racial and ethnic comparisons of success.

Additionally chapters four and five focus on the spouses and children of Asian Indian elites. Much of the data that those chapters are based on comes from interviews with the elites themselves about their spouses and children or participant observation where I had interacted with them. While the chapters of this dissertation focus on the culture of success as it pertains to Asian Indian elites, adding how their spouses and children feel about their roles would make the arguments of those chapters more convincing. Also this would foster a deeper understanding of their mobility and roles in the culture of success. This requires additional in-depth interviews with the spouses and children of the elites at the heart of this study.

In chapter four, I focus on the relationship capital that spouses bring to Asian Indian elites. A future study might examine their marriage markets which intriguing, global, and often virtual. For example, what is the role of global online matrimonial services in the culture of success for Asian Indians? With all these directions for future research, misconceptions about Asian Indians elites may be a thing of the past in the decades to come.

Glossary

Asian Indians: People from the subcontinent of India. Data from the 2000 US Census reveal that Asian Indians are the third largest Asian ethnic group in the United States. While the 1965 Hart-Cellar Act and 1990 Immigration and Nationality Act brought in a highly educated cohort of migrants, the social class differences within the Asian Indian ethnic group are wide. Nevertheless, the majority of Asian Indians (seventy-seven percent) are employed in managerial, professional, technical, sales, and administrative occupations. Fifty-eight percent hold bachelors degrees or higher, in comparison to twenty percent of the US population. Other scholars often refer to Asian Indians as South Asians—a broader category including people from India, Pakistan, Bangladesh, Sri Lanka, Nepal, or Burma.

Assimilation: The etymology of this word is Latin and means to become part of. In its popular usage assimilation refers to the process of Americanization and Anglo-Conformity. As a social scientific concept, there is no consensus, single paradigm, or all encompassing model of assimilation. While debated, in the social sciences assimilation refers to the subtle process of incorporation into the common life of the mainstream group. Based on existing research, the modal pattern of the first generation is accommodation, while for the second generation migrants it is assimilation. This study unpacks the assimilation of high skilled migrants and problematizes this concept.

Corporate Culture: The shared rules governing cognitive and affective aspects of membership in an organization and the means whereby they are shaped and expressed (Kunda 1992:9). This includes the philosophy, values, behaviors, dress codes, etcetera that constitute the policies of a corporation. Communication and leadership skills or the "white male leadership model" are key components of mainstream American corporate culture (Cabezas et al. 1986; Kunda 1992; Schein 1985; Woo 2000).

Cultural Capital: Distinctive tastes and lifestyles that serve as status markers which simultaneously structure inclusion and exclusion (Passeron and Bourdieu 1977; Lamont 1992). Cultural capital includes linguistic competence, command of high culture, displays of cultivated dispositions, level of education, intelligence, and self-actualization. Thus assimilation is the process of social capital formation and identity is its manifestation.

High-Skilled Migrants: People with qualifications as managers, executives, professionals, technicians or similar, who move within the internal labor markets of transnational corporations and international organizations, or who seek employment through international labor markets for scarce skills. Many countries like the United States welcome such migrants and have special skilled and business migration programs to encourage them to come. In the United States, the 1965 Hart-Cellar Act, 1990 Immigration and Nationality Act, and the H-1B Visa Program provided migration opportunities for high-skilled professionals and their families.

Identity: Identity is socially constructed through boundaries that constitute the self. Identity is a manifestation of social capital. People draw subjective boundaries on the basis of socioeconomic, moral, and cultural lines to distinguish themselves from others (Goffman 1959; Passeron and Bourdieu 1977; Cornell and Hartmann; Lamont 1992). Race, ethnicity, immigration status, caste, gender, occupation, and organization are examples of domains that identity can often overlap.

Mediating Organizations: These institutional sites of interaction between newcomers and established residents are where social capital is formed. Mediating organizations include educational institutions, places of residence, the workplace and can construct, shape, and constrain interrelations between recent migrants and established residents (Lamphere et al. 1992)

Skilled Speakers International: Non-profit, international, profession development organization that provides training in communication and leadership skills to the community. While founded in 1924 in Southern California, the organization now boasts over 9,300 clubs in over eighty countries. The most significant growth in the organization of Skilled Speakers International is in onsite corporate sponsored clubs. More than one thousand major corporations sponsor onsite corporate sponsored clubs suggesting that they are becoming institutionalized within corporate America. Two Skilled Speakers Clubs are the research sites for this study: a specialized club for Asian Indian professionals in Southern California and the same type of club in the Silicon Valley.

Social Capital: The capacity to command concrete or intangible resources on an individual and group level by virtue of membership in social networks or social institutions (Loury 1977; Bourdieu 1986; Portes and Zhou 1992; Portes 1995). Social Capital is manifest though sets of obligations, shared norms, and mutual trust necessary to accomplish actions. Based on this definition, identity is constructed through social capital and assimilation is the process of social capital formation.

Social Networks: Relationships that crate links between groups of people through occupational, familial, cultural, or emotional ties. Whether weak or strong, social networks are the primary means to access social capital and can constrain and enable an individual's goals (Dalton 1959; Granovetter 1973; Portes 1995).

Interview Instruments

INTERVIEW INSTRUMENT i

EXPLAIN INFORMED CONSENT DOCUMENT; OBTAIN SIGNATURE; PROVIDE R A COPY

I am conducting this confidential study to obtain more information on how high skilled migrants adapt to their surroundings. The interview will take approximately one-hour. In order to get your exact words, I need to take the interview. Is that okay?

Section 1: Background

Tell me the story of your life: where were you born, where did you grow up, and how did you end up here?[55]
Where are your parents from?
Where did you attend school/college?
How did you end up in the United States?
What is your marital status?
How did you meet your spouse?

---

[55] Question taken from the Russell Sage Foundation, "Immigration, Racial/Ethnic Diversity, and Multiracial Identification," 2001-2004, (Co-Principal Investigators Frank D. Bean and Jennifer Lee)

Section 2: Migration Experience

The following questions deal with your migration experience.
[*If R is a second generation migrant and was born in the US, ask
section 2 in reference to their parents—substitute "your parents" for
"you"*]

How long did you live in __________?
What region of India are you from?
What is your caste?
What does caste mean to you?
How did you learn about it?
Are caste issues salient here in the US?
Did you work when you lived in __________?
What was your job title when you lived in __________?
What kind of work did you do?
What were your job responsibilities?
When did you migrate to the US?
How did you decide to come?
Did you migrate alone?
How did that person affect your decision to come to the US?
How did you get to the US?
How did you end up in __________?
How long have you lived here?
When did you move here?
Did you receive any help from family, friends, or organizations when
migrating here?
What sort of help did you receive?
Why didn't you receive any help?
After you arrived in the US, did any of your friends or family migrate
here?
How many migrated here?
What is your relation with those that migrated here after you arrived?
Did you sponsor or support your migrating friends or family?
How are they doing financially and socially?

Section 3: Work Environment

What is your current employment status?
Where do/did you work?
Describe the culture/mission statement of the company that you worked for.
What is your job title now?
Are you doing the same type of work that you did __________?
How would you compare your job here to the one that you had in __________?
Does the company that you work for have an onsite Skilled Speakers International?
Have you ever attended meetings there?
How does it compare to your home club?
Why do you attend the home club instead of corporate?
Who are your close colleagues at work?
Are your colleagues promoted at the same rate as you?
Who are your supervisors?
How do you get along with your supervisors?
Do you think that there are benefits to being Asian Indian and working in this sector?
What are some stereotypes of Asian Indians? Have you personally encountered any? Do they apply to you?
Have you experienced any hostility or discrimination because you are Asian Indian? Can you recall the last time that this happened? What exactly happened? How do you strategize around this?
How does __________ compare with other regions that you have worked in?
Has the downturn affected your experience in the US?
Has membership in Skilled Speakers International impacted your career in any way?
How so?

Section 4: Self-Employment

Tell me a little bit about your business/company.
What is the name of your business/company?
What does your company do?

How long has your company been open?
Were you employed before opening your business/company?
Are you doing the same type of work that you did when you were working for an employer?
What prompted you to open your own business?
How would you compare being self-employed to working for an employer?
What kinds of funds did you use to start your business?
How would you describe the mission/culture of your business/company?
How many people do you employ?
What are the job titles of your employees?
What are their racial backgrounds?
Are any immigrants?
How do immigrants and native born workers interact?
How would you compare the immigrants that you have employed to those that are native-born Americans?
Did your friends or colleagues help you with your business venture?
Did you seek the help of professional networks?
Has membership in Skilled Speakers International and this club in particular impacted your business in any way?

Section 5: Professional Networks

How did you find out about the club?
How long were you a guest at club meetings?
What prompted you to become a member?
Have you attended meetings at other clubs?
Why did you choose this club in particular?
What do you think the mission of Skilled Speakers is?
Is it being realized?
Does anything beyond this go on at the club?
Probe for specific examples.
What are the benefits to being a member of the club?
Have you experienced any of these benefits?
Why is the club named_________________________________?
What does it mean to be a _____________________?
Is there a need for specialized clubs like this one in the professional community?

Are you a member of any other organization?
Which ones and what do you do?
So how long have you been a member of this club?
How often do you attend club meetings and events?
What was the subject matter of your icebreaker speech? Why did you choose this topic?
What was the subject matter of your speeches that followed? Why did you choose these topics?
Have you ever participated in contests?
Probe for what they did & interaction with other clubs and their members.
What subject matters do other members speak on?
Describe the members of the club.
Why do you think Non-Asian Indians and non-Immigrants become members of the club?
Do you know what their occupations are?
Do you know how they found out about the club?
Who are you closest to in the club?
Are there any members that you prefer not to associate with? Who? Why or how come?
Are there any members that you feel hostile towards?
Are there any members that you are indifferent towards?
Are there any members that you feel sympathy for?
Are there any members who think that they are better than you?
Are there any members who think they are inferior to you?
Are there any members whom you would like to associate with?
Who is your mentor?
Are you a mentor for any members?
Do you interact with any members outside of the club?
Have you ever brought guests to the club?
Why do you think some guests don't become members?
Why do some members stop coming to the club?
Can you recall any examples?
What are your expectations of the club?
What are your expectations of the members?
What are the benefits of being a Skilled Speaker?
Have members assisted you with your professional career or business ventures?
Are there any challenges to being a Skilled Speaker?

What do you think the members' frames of reference are: US Culture; Indian Culture; Both, or Neither?

Section 6: Identity

How do you racially/ethnically identify?
How important is it to you to identify as_____________?
How do other people identify you?
Do you encounter barriers in your life because you are _____________?
What kinds of barriers? How do you get around them? Is Skilled Speakers a way to get around them?
Does your occupation impact your identity? How so?
What does it mean to be a Skilled Speaker?
Do you identify as a Skilled Speaker?
Is identifying as a Skilled Speaker important to you? Why or why not?
Has becoming a Skilled Speaker changed how you identify? (how so?)
How do other Skilled Speakers identify you? How do you feel about their identification of you?

Section 7: Demographics

What is your date of birth? So that makes you how old?
How many years of education have you completed?
What is your annual household income? (Show Respondent Option Card)
Let's look forward: Where do you see yourself in terms of your career or socially in the next five years? How do you plan to achieve your goals?

May I contact you if I have additional questions?

INTERVIEW INSTRUMENT ii

EXPLAIN INFORMED CONSENT DOCUMENT; OBTAIN VERBAL

I am conducting this confidential study to understand the meaning of success for high skilled migrants and how they adapt to their surroundings.   The interview will take approximately one-hour. In order to get your exact words, I need to tape the interview. Is that okay with you?

Section 1: Work Environment

What do you do here at…?
How long have you worked here?
Where did you work prior to this?
How many people do you work with? *(PROBE PARTICIPANT)*
What do you look for in a job candidate when you make a hiring decision?
Probe for communication and leadership skills
Do you like/dislike the people you hire?
DESCRIBE YOUR TYPICAL WORK DAY
HOW MUCH TIME DO YOU SPEND
COMMUNICATING/SPEAKING—PROBE IN WHAT CAPACITY
Do you think that there are any benefits to being Asian Indian and working in this sector? (probe participant for details: ask if they can recall the last time that it helped them)
IF NOT VOL: What are some stereotypes of Asian Indians? Have you personally encountered any of them? Do they apply to you?
Have you ever experienced any hostility or discrimination because you are Asian Indian? Can you recall the last time that happened? What exactly happened? How do you strategize around this?
Do you have any professional or personal role models…?
Are you a member of any professional, community, or cultural organizations?
Have you heard of ______________? (IF NOT VOL: Have you ever thought about joining? Why/Why Not)

Section 2: Background

Where were you born? Where did you grow up?
Probes:
Where are your parents from?
Where did you attend school/college?
How did you end up in the United States?
What is your marital status—
How did you meet your (spouse)? How long have you been married?
What is your spouse's line of work?
Do you have children?
What do they do…?
Do you think your children are (*or will be*) as successful as you are…?
Are you happy…?
What about your children & spouse?
How long did you live in (COUNTRY OF BIRTH)?
________MONTH(S)__________YEAR(S)
What region of India are (you, your parents, your ancestors) from?
What is your caste?
[DEF: "What does caste mean to you or your family?" "How did you learn about what caste is?"]
[IF NOT VOL: Are caste issues salient here in the United States? (Why do you think that is?) Do you encounter and stereotypes about caste?]

Probes:
When did you migrate to the United States?
How did you decide to come to the United States?
Did you migrate alone?
How did that person affect your decision to migrate to the United States?
How did you get to the United States? (ask them about their immigration status then and now)
How long you lived here?
Why did you move here?
Probes:
How many migrated here?
What is your relation with those that migrated here after you arrived?
Did you sponsor of support your migrating friends or family?

Ask about migration cohort—friends or colleagues that came at the same time or schoolmates-
How are they doing financially and socially?

Section 3: Demographics

What is your date of birth? So you're how old now?
How many years of education have you completed?
What is your annual household income?
SHOW RESPONDENT RESPONSE OPTION CARD; ASK RESPONDENT TO TELL YOU THE LETTER THAT CORRESPONDS TO THEIR INCOME; CIRCLE RESPONSE OPTION
Let's look forward. Where do you see yourself, in terms of your career or socially, in the next five years? (How do you plan to achieve these career or social goals?)

Higher Education Among Asian Indians by Region and Gender

Table: Higher Education Among Asian Indians by Region and Gender

Region	College Graduate (%)	Advanced Degree (%)
M a l e s		
Silicon Valley	31.2	36.4
Los Angeles	23.6	28.9
F e m a l e s		
Silicon Valley	28.5	23.8
Los Angeles	24.9	16.4

Source: 2000 1% IPUMS (weighted)

References

Alarcon, Rafael. 1999. "Recruitment Processes Among Foreign-Born Engineers and Scientists in Silicon Valley." *American Behavioral Scientist* 42 (9): 1381-1397.

Alba, Richard. 1990. *Ethnic Identity: Transformation of White America*. New Haven, Conn.: Yale University Press.

Alba, Richard and Victor Nee. 2003. *Remaking the American Mainstream: Assimilation and Contemporary Immigration*. Cambridge: Harvard University Press.

Ammot, T. L. and J. A. Matthaei. 1991. *Race, Gender, & Work: A Multicultural Economic History of Women in the United States*. Boston: South End Press.

Aptekar, Sofya. 2009. "Organizational life and political incorporation of two Asian immigrant groups: A case study." *Ethnic and Racial Studies* 32(9): 1511-1533.

Asian Americans for Community Involvement. 1993. *Qualified, But .... A Report on Glass Ceiling Issues Facing Asian Americans in Silicon Valley*. San Jose, California: AACI.

Bagchi, Ann D. *Making Connections: A Study of Networking Among Immigrant Professionals*. New York: LFB Scholarly Publishing LLC.

Barkan, Elliot Robert. 1992. *Asian and Pacific Islander Migration to the United States: A Model of New Global Patterns*. Westport, CT: Greenwood Publishing Group, INC.

Batalova, Jeanne. 2006. *Skilled Immigrant and Native Workers in the United States: The Economic Competition Debate and Beyond*. Texas: LFB Scholarly Publishing.

Bean, Frank D. and Gillian Stevens. 2004. "Assimilation Redux." *Contemporary Sociology* 33:404-407.

Bean, Frank D., Gillian Stevens, and Susan Wierzbicki. 2003. "The New Immigrants and Theories of Incorporation." Pp. 94-113 in *America's Newcomers and the Dynamics of Diversity*, edited by F. D. B. a. G. Stevens. New York: Russell Sage Foundation.

Bean, Frank D., Jennifer Lee, Jeanne Batalova, and Sabeen Sandhu. 2004. "Immigration and the Black-White Color Line in the United States," *Review of the Black Political Economy.* Special Issue on *The Impact of Immigration on African Americans* 31 (1-2): 43-76.

Becker, Howard S. 1984. *Writing for Social Scientists: How to Start and Finish you Thesis, Book, or Article.* Chicago: University of Chicago Press.

Behera, Navnita Chadha. 2006. "Introduction." Pp. 21-71 in *Gender, Conflict, and Migration*, edited by N. C. Behera. Thousand Oaks: Sage Publications.

Borjas, George J. 1985. "Assimilation, Changes in Cohort Quality, and the Earnings of Immigrants," *Journal of Labor Economics* 3: 463-489.

Brubaker, Rogers. 2001. "The Return of Assimilation? Changing Perspectives on Immigration and Its Sequels in France, Germany, and the United States." *Ethnic and Racial Studies* 24: 531-548.

Bourdieu, Pierre. 1985. "The Forms of Capital," in *Handbook of Theory and Research for the Sociology of Education*, edited by John G. Richardson. New York: Greenwood: 241-258.

Bourdieu, Pierre and Jean-Claude Passeron. 1977. *Reproduction in Education, Society and Culture*. Translated by R. Nice. Beverly Hills: Sage Publication.

Bozorgmehr, Mehdi. 1997. "Internal Ethnicity: Iranians in Los Angeles." *Sociological Perspectives* 40:387-408.

Bretell, Caroline. 2000. *Migration Theory: Talking Across Disciplines.* New York: Routeledge.

Brown, John Seeley and Paul Duguid. 2000. "Mysteries of the Region: Knowledge Dynamics in Silicon Valley." Pp. 16-39 in *The Silicon Valley Edge: A Habitat for Innovation and Entrepreneurship*, edited by C.-M. Lee, W. F. Miller, M. G. Hancock, and H. S. Rowen. Stanford: Stanford University Press.

Burt, Ronald S. 1992. *Structural Holes*. Cambridge: Harvard
    University Press.
Cabezas, Amando, Tse Ming Tam, Brenda M. Lowe, Anna Wong, and
    Kathy Owyang Turner. 1989. "Empirical Study of Barriers to
    Upward Mobility of Asian Americans in the San Francisco
    Bay Area." in *Frontiers of Asian American Studies: Writing,
    Research, and Commentary*, edited by R. E. Gail M. Nomura,
    Stephen H. Sumida, and Russell C. Leong. Pullman:
    Washington State University Press.
Castilla, Emilio J., Hokyu Hwang, Ellen Granovetter, and Mark
    Granovetter. 2000. "Social Networks in the Silicon Valley."
    Pp. 218-247 in *The Silicon Valley Edge: A Habitat for
    Innovation and Entrepreneurship*, edited by C.-M. Lee, W. F.
    Miller, M. G. Hancock, and H. S. Rowen. Stanford: Stanford
    University Press.
Chang, Lucie and Philip Yang. 1996. "Asians: The 'Model Minority'
    Deconstructed," in *Ethnic Los Angeles* eds. Roger Waldinger
    and Medhi Bozorgmehr. New York: Russell Sage
    Foundation: 320-323.
Chiswick, Barry R. 1977. "Sons of Immigrants: Are they at an
    Earnings Disadvantage?" *American Economic Review* 67:
    376-380.
Chow, Sue. 2000. "The Significance of Race in the Private Sphere:
    Asian Americans and Spousal Preferences." *Sociological
    Inquiry* 70:1-29.
Cohen, Stephen S. and Gary Fields. 2000. "Social Capital and Capital
    Gains: An Examination of Social Capital in Silicon Valley."
    Pp. 190-217 in *Understanding Silicon Valley: The Anatomy of
    an Entrepreneurial Region*, edited by M. Kenney. Stanford:
    Stanford University Press.
Coleman, J.S. 1985. "Social Capital in the Creation of Human
    Capital," *American Journal of Sociology* 94 (8): 95-121.
Cornell, Stephen and Douglas Hartmann. 2007. *Ethnicity and Race:
    Making Identities in a Changing World*. Second Edition.
    Thousand Oaks, California: Pine Forge Press.
Cornelius, Wayne A., Thomas J. Espenshade, and Idean Salehyan.
    2001. *The International Migration of the Highly Skilled.
    Demand, Supply, and Development Consequences in Sending*

and Receiving Countries. La Jolla: Center for Comparative Immigration Studies: University of California, San Diego.

Coser, Lewis A.1974. *Greedy Institutions: Patterns of Undivided Commitment.* New York: Free Press.

Dalton, M. 1959. *Men who Manage.* New York: Wiley.

Dasgupta, S. S. 1986. "Marching to a Different Drummer? Sex Roles of Asian Indian Women in the United States." *Women and Therapy* 5:297-311.

Davis, Kingsley. 1941. "Intermarriage in a Caste Society." *American Anthropologist* 43:376-395.

Denzin, Norman K. 1989. *The Research Act.* Englewood Cliffs: Prentice-Hall.

Dinnerstein, M. 1992. *Women Between Two Worlds: Midlife Reflections on Work and Family.* Philadelphia: Temple University Press.

Dreyer, N. A., N. F. Woods, and S. A. James. 1981. "ISRO: A Scale to Measure Sex-Role Orientation." *Sex Roles* 7:173-188.

Durkheim, Emile. 1893. *The Division of Labor in Society.* New York: Free Press.

Easterday, Lois, Diana Papademas, Laura Schorr, and Catherine Valentine. 1977. "The Making of a Female Researcher: Role Problems in the Field." *Urban Life* 6:333-348.

Ellis and Lowell. 2003. "The Outlook in 2003 for Information Technology Workers in the USA." *The IT Workforce Data Project.* Institute for the Study of International Migration: Georgetown University.

Emerson, Robert M., Rachel I. Fretz, and Linda L. Shaw. 1995. *Writing Ethnographic Fieldnotes.* Chicago: University of Chicago Press.

English-Luek, J.A. 2002. *Cultures@SiliconValley.* Stanford: Stanford University Press.

Espiritu, Yen Le. 2000. *Asian American Women and Men: Labor, Laws, and Love.* Walnut Creek: AltaMira Press.

Feagin, Joe R., Gideon Sjoberg, and Anthony M. Orum. 1991. *A Case for the Case Study.* Chapel Hill: University of North Carolina Press.

Fernandez, Marilyn. 1998. "Asian Indian Americans in the Bay Area and the Glass Ceiling." *American Behavioral Scientist* 41:119-140.

Fernandez, Marilyn and Laura Nichols. 2002. "Bridging and Bonding Social Capital: Pluralistic Ethnic Relations in Silicon Valley." *International Journal of Sociology and Social Policy* 22:104-121.

Foner, Nancy, Ruben G. Rumbaut, and Alejandro Portes. 2000. *Immigration Research for a New Century.* New York: Russell Sage Foundation.

Fugita, Stephen S. and David O'Brien. 1991. *Japanese American Ethnicity: The Persistence of Community.* Seattle: University of Washington.

Gans, Herbert. 1979. "Symbolic Ethnicity: The Future of Ethnic Groups and Cultures in America." *Ethnic and Racial Studies* 2:1-20.

-----. 1992. "Second Generation Decline: Scenarios for the Economic and Ethnic Futures of Post-1965 American Immigrants." *Ethnic and Racial Studies* 15: 173-192.

Geer, Blanche. 1964. "First Days in the Field," Pp. 322-344 in *Sociologists at Work: Essays on the Craft of Social Research,* Edited by Phillip Hammond. New York: Basic Books.

Geertz, Clifford. 1976. *The Interpretation of Cultures.* New York: Basic Books.

Gerstel, Naomi and Natalia Sarkisian. 2006. "Marriage: The Good, the Bad, and the Greedy." *Contexts* 5:16-21.

Ghadially, R. 1988. *Women in Indian Society.* New Dehli: Sage Press.

Gibson, Magaret. 1988. *Accommodation without Assimilation: Sikh Immigrants in an American High School.* Ithaca and London: Cornell University Press.

Glaser, Barney G. 1992. *Basics of Grounded Theory: Emergence vs Forcing.* Mill Valley: Sociology Press.

Glaser, Barney G. and Anselm L. Strauss. 1967. *The Discovery of Grounded Theory: Strategies for Qualitative Research.* Chicago: Adline.

Glazer, Nathan and Daniel Patrick Moynihan. 1970. Beyond the Melting Pot: The Negroes, Puerto Ricans, Jews, Italians, and Irish of New York City. Cambridge: MIT Press.

Goffman, Erving. 1959. *The Presenation of Self in Everyday Life.* New York: Doubleday.

—. 1971. *Relations in Public: Microstudies of the Public Order.* San Francisco: Harper Colophon Books.

Gold, Liza H. 2004. *Sexual Harassment: Psychiatric Assessment in Employment Litigation*. Washington, D.C.: American Psychiatric Publishing, Inc.

Golde, Peggy. 1986. *Women in the Field: Anthropological Experiences*. Berkeley: University of California Press.

Goodwin, Jeff and Ruth Horowitz. 2002. "Introduction: The Methodological Strengths and Dilemmas of Qualitative Sociology." *Qualitative Sociology* 25:33-47.

Gordon, Milton. 1964. *Assimilation in American Life: The Role of Race, Religion, and National Origins*. New York: Oxford University Press.

Granovetter, Mark. 1985. "Economic Action and Social Structure: The Problem of Embeddedness." *American Journal of Sociology*: 481-510.

Gupta, S., M.A. Shah, and M.A. Beg. 1982. "Educational and Socioeconomic Status as Determinants of Indian Women's Attitudes Towards Equality of Women." *The Journal of Social Psychology* 118:139-140.

Halter, Marilyn. 2000. *Shopping for Identity: The Marketing of Ethnicity*. New York: Schocken Books.

Hartmann, Heidi. 1984. "The Unhappy Marriage of Marxism and Feminism: Towards a More Progressive Union." in *Feminist Frameworks: Alternative Accounts of the Relations Between Women and Men*, edited by A. J. a. P. Rotenberg. New York: McGraw Hill.

Hertz, Rosanna and Jonathan B. Imber. 1995. *Studying Elites Using Qualitative Methods*. Thousand Oaks: Sage Publication.

Ho, Pensri. 2003. "Performing the Oriental: Professionals and the Asian Model Minority Myth." *Journal of Asian American Studies* 6 (2): 149-176.

Hochschild, A. 1989. *The Second Shift*. New York: Avon.

Jackall, R. 1988. *Moral Mazes*. New York: Oxford University Press.

Jensen, Joan M. 1988. *Passage from India: Asian Indian Immigrants in North America*. New Haven: Yale University Press.

Johnson, J. M. 1975. *Doing Field Research*. New York: Free Press.

Kanter, Rosabeth Moss. 1975. "Women and the Structure of Organizations: Explorations in Theory and Behavior." Pp. 34-74 in *Another Voice: Feminist Perspectives on Social Life and Social Science*, edited by M. M. a. R. M. Kanter. New York: Double Day.

—. 1977. *Men and Women of the Corporation.* New York: Basic Books.

Katz, Jack. 1997. "Ethnography's Warrants." *Sociological Methods Research* 25:391-423.

Koch, James L. and Ross Miller. 2001. "Community: A Comparison of the Silicon Valley-Pennisula Region with the National Social Capital Benchmark Results." Center for Science, Technology, and Society at Santa Clara University.

Kunda, Gideon. 1992. *Engineering Culture: Control and Committment in a High-Tech Corporation.* Philadelphia: Temple University Press.

Kurzman, Charles, Chelise Anderson, Clinton Key, Youn Ok Lee, Mairead Maloney, Alexis Silver, and Maria W. Van Ryn. 2007. "Celebrity Status." *Sociological Theory* 25:347-367.

Lamont, Michéle. 1992. *Money, Morals, and Manners: The Culture of French and the American Upper-Middle Class.* Chicago: University of Chicago Press.

Lamphere, Louise. 1993. *Structuring Diversity: Ethnographic Perspectives on the New Immigration.* Chicago: University of Chicago Press.

Lee, Jennifer. 1999. "Immigrant and African American Competition: Jewish, Korean, and African American Entrepreneurs." *American Behavioral Scientist* 42:1398-1416.

—. 2002. *Civility in the City: Blacks, Jews, and Koreans in Urban America.* Cambridge: Harvard University Press.

Lee, Jennifer and Frank D. Bean. 2010. *The Diversity Paradox: Immigration and the Color Line in 21st Century America.* New York: The Russell Sage Foundation.

Levy, Steven 2008. "On the Upward Slide." *Newsweek*, March 24.

Light, Ivan and Steven J. Gold. 2000. *Ethnic Economies.* Academic Press.

Lin, Nan. 2001. "Building a Network Theory of Social Capital." Pp. 3-30 in *Social Capital: Theory and Research*, edited by K. C. Nan Lin, Ronald S. Burt. New York: Aldine De Gruyter.

Loftland, John, David Snow, Leon Anderson, and Lyn H. Loftland. 2006. *Analyzing Social Settings: A Guide to Qualitative Observation and Analysis.* United States: Thomson Wadsworth.

Malinowski, Bronislaw. 1967. *A Diary in the Strict Sense of the Term.* New York: Harcourt Brace.

Manalansan, Martin F. 2000. *Cultural Compass: Ethnographic Explorations of Asia America.* Philadelphia: Temple University Press.

Massey, Douglas S. 1981. "Dimensions of the New Immigration to the United States and the Prospects for Assimilation." *Annual Review of Sociology* 7: 57-85.

McDonald, Gerald W. 1981. "Structural Exchange and Marital Interaction." *Journal of Marriage and Family* 43:825-831.

Merton, Robert K. 1987. "Three Fragments from a Sociologist's Notebook: Establishing the Phenomenon, Specified Ignorance, and Strategic Research Materials." *Annual Review of Sociology* 13:1-28.

—. 1995. "Foreward." Pp. vii-xi in *The Economic Sociology of Immigration: Essays on Networks, Ethnicity, and Entrepreneurship*, edited by A. Portes. New York: Russell Sage Foundation.

Merton, Robert M. 1941. "Intermarriage and the Social Structure: Fact and Theory." *Psychiatry* 4:361-374.

Milken Institute. 2003. "High Tech Darwinism." In *Los Angeles Times Magazine* 9 March: 24-25.

Mills, Nicolaus. 1994. *Arguing Immigration: The Debate over the Changing Face of America.* New York: Touchstone.

Morrill, Calvin. 1991. "Conflict Management, Honor, and Organizational Change." *American Journal of Sociology* 97:585-621.

Morrill, Calvin and Gary Alan Fine. 1997. "Ethnographic Contributions to Organizational Sociology." *Sociological Methods Research* 25:424-451.

Nader, Laura. 1970. "From Anguish to Exultation." Pp. 97-116 in *Women in the Field: Anthropological Experiences*, edited by P. Golde. Berkeley: University of California Press.

Nagel, Joane. 1996. *American Indian Ethnic Renewal: Red Power and the Resurgence of Identity and Culture.* New York: Oxford University Press.

Neckerman, Kathryn M., Prudence Carter, and Jennifer Lee. 1999. "Segmented Assimilation and Minority Cultures of Mobility." *Ethnic and Racial Studies* 22 (6): 945-965.

Okihiro, Gary Y. 1994. *Margins and Mainstreams: Asians in American History and Culture.* Washington: University of Washington Press.

Olsen, F. 1992. "Does Enough Work Make Women Free?" *Indian Journal of Social Work* LIII 4:599-610.

Park, Lisa Sun-Hee. 2005. *Consuming Citizenship: The Children of Asian Immigrant Entrepreneurs.* Stanford: Stanford University Press.

Park, Robert E. and Ernest W. Burgess. 1921. *Introduction to the Science of Sociology.* Chicago: University of Chicago Press

Paxton, Pamela and Anthony Mughan. 2006. "What's to Fear from Immigrants? Creating an Assimilationist Threat Scale." *Political Psychology* 27(4): 549-568.

Pellow, David Naguib and Lisa Sun-Hee Park. 2002. *The Silicon Valley of Dreams: Environmental Justice, Immigrant Workers, and the High-Tech Global Economy.* New York: New York University Press.

Pepitone, Julianne. 2011. "Silicon Valley fights to keep its diversity data secret." *CNNMoneyTech. 9 November.* http://www.money.cnn.com/2011/11/09/technology/diversity_ silicon_valley/index.htm

Peterson, V. Spike and Anne Sisson Runyan. 1999. *Global Gender Issues.* Boulder: Westview Press.

Portes, Alejandro. 1995. "Economic Sociology and the Sociology of Immigration: A Conceptual Overview." Pp. 1-41 in *The Economic Sociology of Immigration: Essays on Networks, Ethnicity, and Entrepreneurship*, edited by A. Portes. New York: Russell Sage Foundation.

—. 1998. "Social Capital: Its Origins and Applications in Modern Sociology." *Annual Review of Sociology* 24:12-37.

Portes, Alejandro and Rubén G. Rumbaut. 2001. *Legacies: The Story of the Immigrant Second Generation.* Berkeley: University of California Press.

Portes, Alejandro and Min Zhou. 1992. "Gaining the Upper Hand: Economic Mobility Among Immigrant and Domestic Minorities," *Ethnic and Racial Studies* 15 (4): 491-522.

-----. 1993. "The New Second Generation: Segmented Assimilation and Its Variants Among Post-1965 Immigrant Youth," *Annals*

of the American Academy of Political and Social Science 530:
74-98.

Powdermaker, Hortense. 1966. *Stranger and Friend*. New York: W. W.
Norton.

Prashad, Vijay. 2000. *The Karma of Brown Folk*. Minneapolis:
University of Minnesota Press.

Putnam, Robert. 1995. "Bowling Alone: America's Declining Social
Capital." *Journal of Democracy* 6:65-78.

-----. 2000. *Bowling Alone: The Collapse and Revival of American
Community*. New York: Simon and Schuster.

Ragin, Charles C. and Howard S. Becker. 1992. *What is a Case?
Exploring the Foundations of Social Inquiry*. Cambridge:
Cambridge University Press.

Reitz, Jeffrey G. 1980. *The Survival of Ethnic Groups*. Toronto:
McGraw Hill Ryerson Limited.

Rumbaut, Rubén G. 2011. "Assimilation's Bumpy Road." Pp. 184-219
in *American Democracy and the Pursuit of Equality*, edited by
Merlin Chowkwanyun and Randa Serhan. Boulder, Colorado:
Paradigm Publishers.

-----. 2008. "Immigration's Complexities, Assimilation's Discontents."
Contexts: Understanding People in their Social World 7:72.

-----. 1999. "Assimilation and its Discontents: Ironies and Paradoxes."
Pp. 172-195 in *The Handbook of International Migration:
The American Experience*, edited by P. K. Charles Hirschman,
and Josh DeWind. New York: Russell Sage Foundation.

Sacks, K. 1974. "Engels Revisited: Women, The Organization or
Production and Private Property." in *Women, Culture, and
Society*, edited by M. R. a. L. Lamphere. Stanford: Stanford
University Press.

Sahoo, Ajaya, Dave Sangha, and Melissa Kelly. 2010. "From
'temporary migrants' to 'permanent residents': Indian H-1B
visa holders in the United States." *Asian Ethnicity* 11(3): 293-
309.

Sandhu, Sabeen. 2002. "The Skills Match Hypothesis: Asian Indian
Immigrants in the Silicon Valley," *Unpublished Masters
Thesis*. Irvine: The University of California.

-----.2003. "Divergent Fortunes: An Intragroup Comparison of
Occupational Mobility Among Asian Indians in the Silicon
Valley," *Unpublished Paper Presented at the University of*

California Institute for Labor and Employment Graduate Student Research Conference.

-----.2004. "Instant Karma: The Commercialization of Asian Indian Culture," Pp. 131-141 in *Asian Youth Cultures, Identity, and Ethnicity.* Edited by Min Zhou and Jennifer Lee. New York. Routledge Press.

Saxenian, Annalee. 1994. *Regional Advantage: Culture and Competition in Silicon Valley and Route 128.* Cambridge: Harvard University Press.

—. 2000a. "Networks of Immigrant Entrepreneurs." Pp. 248-268 in *The Silicon Valley Edge: A Habitat for Innovation and Entrepreneurship*, edited by C.-M. Lee, W. F. Miller, M. G. Hancock, and H. S. Rowen. Stanford: Stanford University Press.

—. 2000b. ""The Origins and Dynamics of Production Networks in Silicon Valley"." Pp. 141-162 in Understanding Silicon Valley: The Anatomy of an Entrepreneurial Region, edited by M. Kenney. Stanford: Stanford University Press.

Schein, Edgar H. 1987. "Organizational Culture and Leadership." *Jossey-Bass*: 1-22.

Sheth, Manju. 1995. "Asian Indian Americans." in *Asian Americans: Comparative Trends and Issues*, edited by P. G. Min. Newberry Park: Sage Publications.

Shibutani, Tamotsu and Kian Kwan. 1965. *Ethnic Stratification.* New York: MacMillan.

Siisianinen, Martti. 2000. "Two Concepts of Social Capital: Bourdieu vs. Putnam." in *ISTR Fourth International Conference.* Trinity College, Dublin, Ireland.

Simmel, Georg. 1950. *The Sociology of Georg Simmel.* Glencoe: The Free Press.

Singleton, Royce A. and Bruce C. Straits. 1999. *Approaches to Social Research.* New York: Oxford University Press.

Sircar, Arpana. 2000. *Work Roles, Gender Roles, and Asian Indian Immigrant Women in the United States.* New York: The Edwin Mellen Press.

Snow, David A. and Leon Anderson. 1991. "Researching the Homeless: The Characteristic Features and Virtues of the Case Study." Pp. 148-173 in *A Case for the Case Study,* edited by G. S. Joe R. Feagin, and Anthony M. Orum. Chapel Hill: University of North Carolina Press.

—. 1993. *Down on Their Luck: A Study of Homeless Street People.* Berkeley: University of California Press.

Snow, David A., Robert D. Benford, and Leon Anderson. 1986. "Fieldwork Roles and Informational Yield: A Comparison of Alternative Settings and Roles." *Urban Life* 15:337-408.

Snow, David A., Calvin Morrill, and Leon Anderson. 2003. "Linking Ethnography and Theoretical Development." *Ethnography* 2:181-200.

Spradley, J. 1980. *Participant Observation.* New York: Holt, Rinehart and Winston.

Springer, Richard. 2006. "Potential of Women Migrants 'Largely Ignored'." Pp. 1 in *India West.* Fremont, California.

-----. 2012. "Asians Underrepresented on Fortune 500 Boards." Pp. B1-B4 in *India West.* Fremont, California.

Stack, Carol B. 1974. *All Our Kin: Strategies for Survival in a Black Community.* New York: Harper and Row.

Stake, Robert E. 1978. "The Case Study Method of Social Inquiry." *Educational Researcher* 7:5-8.

Sun-Hee, Park. Lisa. 2005. *Consuming Citizenship: Children of Asian Immigrant Entrepreneurs.* Stanford: Stanford University Press.

Swift, Mike. 2010. "Five Silicon Valley companies fought release of employment data, and won." *San Jose Mercury News* 14 February. http://www.mercurynews.com/ci_14382477?lADID

Tang, Joyce. 1993. "The Career Attainment of Caucasian and Asian Engineers." *Sociological Quarterly* 34 (3): 467-496.

Terrazas, Aaron and Cristina Batog. 2010. "Indian Immigrants in the United States." *Migration Information Source.* Washington D.C.: Migration Policy Institute.

Thapan, Meenakshi. 2006. "Series Introduction." Pp. 7-17 in *Gender, Conflict, and Migration*, edited by N. C. Behera. Thousand Oaks: Sage Publications.

Thibodeau, Patrick. 2011. "High-skill visa reform needs action by Congress, Obama says." *Computerworld* 11 October. http://computerworld.com/article/9220740/High_skill_visa_re form_needs_action_by_Congress_Obama_says

Thomas, Robert J. 1995. "Interviewing Important People in Big Companies." Pp. 3-17 in *Studying Elites Using Qualitative*

Methods, edited by R. H. a. J. B. Imber. Thousand Oaks: Sage Publications.

Useem, Michael. 1995. "Reaching Corporate Executives." In *Studying Elites Using Qualitative Methods*. Edited by Rosanna Hertz and Jonathan B. Imber, Thousand Oaks: Sage Publications: 18-39.

Utinova, Anastasia. 2008. "Isolated Housewives." in *San Francisco Chronicle*. San Francisco.

Van Maanen, John. 1988. *Tales of the Field: On Writing Ethnography*. Chicago: University of Chicago Press.

Varghese, Anitha. 2007. "Acculturation, Parental Control, and Adjustment Among Asian Indian Women." *Psychology*, University of North Texas.

Varma, Roli. 2006. *Harbingers of Global Change: India's Techno-Immigrants in the United States*. Lanham: Lexington Books.

Visweswaran, Kamala. 1994. *Fictions of Feminist Ethnography*. Minneapolis: University of Minnesota.

Vo, Linda Trinh. 2000. "Performing Ethnography in Asian American Communities: Beyond the Insider-versus-Outsider Perspective." Pp. 17-39 in *Cultural Compass: Ethnographic Explorations of Asian America,* edited by M. F. M. IV. Philadelphia: Temple University Press.

Vogel, Lise. 1983. *Marxism and the Oppression of Women: Toward a Unity of Theory*. New Brunswick: Rutgers University Press.

Wang, L. Ling-Chi. 2007. "Overrepresentation and Disenfranchisement: Asian Americans in Higher Education." *Amerasia Journal* 33:77-100.

Warner, Lloyd and Leo Srole. 1945. *The Social Systems of American Ethnic Groups.* New Haven: Yale University Press.

Warren, Carol A. B. and Paul K. Rasmussen. 1977. "Sex and Gender in Field Research." *Urban Life* 6:349-368.

Waters, Mary. 1990. *Ethnic Options: Choosing Identities in America*. Berkeley and Los Angeles: University of California Press.

—. 1999. *Black Identities: West Indian Immigrant Dreams and American Realities*. New York and Cambridge: The Russell Sage Foundation & Harvard University Press.

Weber, Max. 1946. *From Max Weber: Essays in Sociology*, Edited by H. H. G. a. C. W. Mills. New York: Oxford University Press.

Woo, Deborah. 2000. *Glass Ceilings and Asian Americans: The New Face of Workplace Barriers.* Walnut Creek: Alta Mira Press.

Yoon, In-Jin. 1997. *On My Own: Korean Businesses and Race Relations in America.* Chicago: University of Chicago Press.

Xenos, Peter, Herbert Barringer, and Michael J. Levin. 1989. "Asian Indians in the United States: A 1980 Census Profile." *East-West Center*, Honolulu.

Zhao, Shanyang. 2001. "Toward A Taxonomy of Copresence." in *Annual Meeting of the American Sociological Association.* Anaheim, CA.

Zhou, Min. 1992. *Chinatown: The Socioeconomic Potential of an Urban Enclave.* Philadelphia: Temple University Press.

Zhou, Min and Carl L. Bankston III. 1998. *Growing Up American: How Vietnamese Children Adapt to Life in the United States.* New York: Russell Sage Foundation.

Zinn, Maxine Baca. 1979. "Field Research in Minority Communities: Ethical, Methodological and Political Observations by an Insider." *Social Problems* 27:209-219.

Index